Handcrafted
CARDS

Handcrafted
CARDS

From Elegant to
Whimsical

60 Distinctive Designs to Make

Paige Gilchrist

LARK
BOOKS

A Division of Sterling Publishing Co., Inc.
New York

This book is dedicated
to the memory of
Margaret Ann Sprague Irwin
who inspired individual creativity in every form of communication.

Art Direction: Dana Irwin
Photography: Sandra Stambaugh
Illustrations: Olivier Rollin, Dana Irwin
Production Assistance: Hannes Charen
Editorial Assistance: Heather Smith, Catharine Sutherland

The Library of Congress has cataloged the hardcover edition as follows:
Gilchrist, Paige.
    Handcrafted cards : from elegant to whimsical, 60 distinctive
designs to make / Paige Gilchrist.
        p.   cm.
    ISBN 1-57990-150-6
    1. Greeting cards. I. Title.
T872.G55 2000
745.594'1--dc21

                                99-38337
                                CIP

10 9

Published by Lark Books, a division of
Sterling Publishing Co., Inc.
387 Park Avenue South, New York, N.Y. 10016

First Paperback Edition 2001
© 2000, Lark Books

Distributed in Canada by Sterling Publishing, c/o Canadian Manda Group, 165 Dufferin Street, Toronto, Ontario, Canada M6K 3H6

Distributed in the United Kingdom by GMC Distribution Services, Castle Place, 166 High Street, Lewes, East Sussex, England BN7 1XU

Distributed in Australia by Capricorn Link (Australia) Pty Ltd., P.O. Box 704, Windsor, NSW 2756 Australia

If you have questions or comments about this book, please contact:
Lark Books, 67 Broadway, Asheville, NC 28801, (828) 253-0467

Manufactured in China

ISBN 13: 978-1-57990-262-9
ISBN 10: 1-57990-150-6 (hardcover) 1-57990-262-6 (paperback)

For information about custom editions, special sales, premium and corporate purchases, please contact Sterling Special Sales Department at 800-805-5489 or specialsales@sterlingpub.com.

CONTENTS

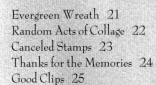
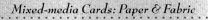

Handmade Cards:
THE MEDIUM AND THE MESSAGE

Think for a minute. When was the last time you watched an incoming fax chugging through your machine and said to yourself, *"How* imaginative; I'll keep this forever." Have you *ever* printed out an e-mail greeting and put it on display because of its beautiful blending of words and images—or saved a birthday wish left on your answering machine because it was so distinctive?

There's much to be said for modern communication. It's fast and efficient—and most of us would prefer not to do without it. There's also a lot of it. Our "in" boxes are multiplying. We're bombarded with messages popping up on our computer screens, scrolling through our fax machines, ringing into our cars, blinking on our answering machines, and piling up in our good old-fashioned mailboxes. Yet, fewer and fewer of those messages are worth saving, let alone savoring. Amid the vast, fast flow of electronic and mass-mailed information, it seems, there's a definite lack of creative, personalized *communication* taking place.

And we miss it. Call it nostalgia. Call it information-age rebellion. But growing numbers of us are deciding that the medium *is* often just as important as the message. We're drawn immediately to hand-lettered envelopes peeking out from under the cable bills and coupon books that make up most stacks of mail. We crave the fun of anticipating what might be inside—and delight in the tactile experience of finding out. We long for the note of thanks, celebration, or news enclosed to surprise us, enchant us, add a dash of artistry to an experience that has become so ordinary.

At the same time, we suspect that the only thing more soothing to our technology-trampled souls than receiving an original, handmade card is creating one ourselves.

A happy birthday,
With love and kisses –
In just 28 days,
You'll be my Mrs.

All my love, Dick

You can take a
lad out of the country
but you can't take
the country out of
him.

Hey Honey
I Will
see You
in a little
while. from
the old Man
M P C
as Ever

Don't forget that you
are planning to visit washington
next spring to see these Japanese
cherry blossoms! –yrs
–H.H.C.

Here's a book that proves the suspicion true. Making your own cards is the most marvelous excuse for playing with the possibilities of color, texture, image, shape—and imagination. If kindergarten was the last time you elbowed your way to a seat at a table full of paints, papers, and glitter and trusted your artistic instincts, you've waited long enough.

The only real rule about making handmade cards is that you share a bit of *yourself* in the process. To help you get started, we asked 22 talented designers to do just that. On the pages that follow, we showcase what they came up with: 60 inspiring, personalized ways to communicate with cards. They gathered some of their favorite supplies—from family photos and garden flowers to trinkets from trips and drawings by grandchildren—and created original works of artistic expression. All you need to transform any one of them into a creation all your own is *your* batch of favorite things.

Their designs incorporate techniques that fall into the just-like-riding-a-bike category (you never forget them)—comfy stuff like cutting, pasting, and sponging on paint. They also introduce you to easy-to-learn others, from stenciling and stamping to using classic folding patterns to make pop-ups.

As you flip through their card designs, which range from elegant to witty, your first thought is likely to be, "*How* imaginative; if I got something like that, I'd keep it forever." Then, in a flash, a second thought takes over, "*I could do that.*"

Which is exactly the idea.

Cardmaking Basics

CHANCES ARE, *if you've celebrated a birthday, observed a holiday, courted (or been courted by) romance, or had or been a parent, greeting cards are a regular and welcome part of your life. What's so terrific about making your own cards is that the tools and techniques involved are just as friendly and familiar as cards themselves.*

Essentially, you need only a blank canvas of a card and a way to adorn it with your message. Now, that can mean making your own paper, fashioning it into cards, and painting elaborate masterpieces to fasten on the front. But it probably doesn't. (And if it does, you'll want to get another book or two.)

More likely, you're interested in blank cards that are ready to go (or a simple method for making your own out of purchased card stock) and original but easy ways to personalize them. If that's the case, here's all you need.

CARDS, ENVELOPES, AND PAPERS

If you'd rather skip measuring and folding and move straight to embellishing, you'll want to start any card-making endeavor with two essential items: a blank, ready-made card and a coordinating envelope. You can find both by the stack in card and stationery stores and art and craft supply shops. Most standard are those referred to as "regular" size (with the cards measuring 5 x 6⁷/₈ inches [12.5 x 17.2 cm] and the envelopes measuring 5¹/₄ x 7¹/₄ inches [13.1 x 18.2 cm]), and "announcement" size (with the cards measuring 3¹/₂ x 4⁷/₈ inches [8.8 x 12.2 cm] and the envelopes measuring 3⁵/₈ x 5¹/₈ inches [9.2 x 13 cm]). If you want something more specialized than the standard sizes, colors, and shapes you find at stationery and craft stores, check with a local print shop about what they can customize for you.

Rather start from scratch? Making your own envelopes and cards is a snap; we show you how in the Techniques section beginning on page 14. What's more, doing so becomes irresistible once you discover the bounty of beautiful papers available for cutting and configuring into whatever shape or size you need.

Paper and Its Weight

You can find paper as thin and delicate as rice paper and as sturdy and unbendable as mat board. It's all technically paper, and any of it can be incorporated into card decor, but for making cards and envelopes themselves, you'll want to choose paper that is in between those two extremes. Paper is categorized by weight (the weight refers to the heaviness of 1,000 sheets), and at any respectable place that sells it, you'll also find a paper lover eager to help you decide which weight and type best meets your needs.

Paper referred to as cover weight or, fittingly, as card stock is just the thing for your cards themselves. Standard commercial greeting cards are typically made with 80-pound (36 kg) cover-weight paper. Postcards are usually created with 65-pound (30 kg) cover-weight paper. Text-weight paper is better for whipping up your own envelopes; card stock is so bulky it tends to buckle under all the folds.

Paper Size

Sheets of card stock and other papers are sold in various sizes. You may find just the color and texture you want in a sheet that measures 7 x 10 inches (17.5 x 25 cm). If so, you can fold it in half, and you've got a (roughly) standard-size greeting card that's 5 x 7 inches (12.5 x 17.2 cm). Letter-size stock that is 8¹/₂ x 10 inches (21.3 x 25 cm) is easy to find, but you'll need to cut it down first if you want to fold it into a standard-size card. Many decorative papers come only in larger sheets. The good news is, cutting your paper into any size or shape that suits your fancy is a simple task. Just remember that if you create cards in unusual sizes, you'll probably have to make envelopes for them, too. (Not to worry, that's also an easy matter; we tell you how in the Techniques section later.)

Paper Sources

Art and craft supply stores stock everything from glossy foil papers to rustic handmade styles full of bark bits and flower fragments. Educational supply stores and stationers are other places to check for eclectic paper collections. And commercial print shops are often happy to sell their "scraps" (client cast-offs that make the rest of us drool) for a nominal price.

Cardmaking tools, clockwise from bottom left: craft knife blades, awl, artist's brushes, glue stick, scissors, rubber cement, spray adhesive, PVA glue, edgers, stencil brushes, bone folder, craft knife, sponge, hole punch, metal ruler, cutting mat.

TOOLS AND SUPPLIES

Craft Knife

A craft knife tops the list of tools that, if lost, any card maker would rush out and replace right away. You'll use yours for everything from cutting out shapes for collages to slicing slots for interesting closures on envelopes. Choose one with replaceable and switchable blades, and you'll always be prepared to make a variety of clean, sharp cuts.

Cutting Mat

If craft knives are so popular, it stands to reason that something to cut upon comes in handy, too. Craft stores sell cutting mats, some complete with complex grid systems. You can also use a common item such as a piece of masonite or linoleum or a plastic kitchen cutting board (a clean one, rather than a cast-off covered with stains, of course!). Simply search for something that won't dull your knife quickly and won't easily retain score marks.

Metal Ruler

This straightedge of choice for card makers everywhere is in demand for a couple of reasons. The metal (unlike wood or plastic) resists the nicks of your craft knife, while the cork backing gently grips the paper you place it on, keeping the ruler from scooting out of position.

Bone Folder

Essential if you're going to create your own blank cards, a bone folder's rounded edge, raked across your fold line, gives you the crispest of creases. The dull side of a dinner knife will do, but there's no reason not to use the ultimate tool when it's as affordable and available (check any art supply store) as a bone folder. In addition, a bone folder is ideal for burnishing any spot you've adhered to another, and its blunt point is perfect for scoring paper.

Scissors, Edgers, and Others

For some cutting jobs you'll find sharp scissors more manageable than a craft knife (there's no official division of tasks here; preferences vary from card-maker to cardmaker). Keep several sizes and types of scissors on hand if you can, from embroidery scissors to little curved manicure scissors. Ideally, your cardmaking scissors should be reserved for card making only—no fabric cutting or flower-stem clipping on the side; you'll dull the blades.

Other cutting tools can leave interesting edges on cards, envelope flaps, and pieces you clip to attach to card surfaces. Try pinking shears for playful zigzags, for example, or paper edgers (available in a wide selection at craft stores) for everything from scalloped to wavy edges. And don't neglect the fun of making mini cutout patterns in your paper. Few actions are as satisfying as squeezing the handles of a hole punch and clicking out little shapes—

especially now that those shapes include not only the standard circle, but jillions of others, from stars and moons to hearts and shamrocks. The positive images you punch out are just as much fun as the holes they create.

Finally, it's not a must-have, but if you're going to be cutting stacks of paper for folding your own cards and envelopes, a paper cutter (with that industrial-strength cutting arm that makes quick, clean slices through multiple pieces at once) is a tool worth adding to your craft table.

Pencils and Pens

There are pens in medium-tip metallic violet and broad paint markers in florescent orange. Pencils come in pastel to primary colors, and you can eas-

ily find everything from paint crayons to watercolor markers. Whether you're shading in flower stems, adding bright accent dots to cutout curlicues, or lettering a greeting in self-styled calligraphy, you won't want to be without a handful of interesting writing implements.

Adhesives

Cardmakers get attached to their favorite products and techniques for gluing. Everyone's got an opinion on the best way to stick one thing to another. Remember: This is art, not science. Here's a rundown of the general consensus on the best adhesives to use—and what best to use them for.

PVA or polyvinyl acetate, common and well-loved, is the trusty white

A selection of card-decoration supplies

An array of materials for decorating cards

craft glue we all used at some point in our childhoods. It's still around, still dries clear, and still holds well for nearly any gluing job. For best results, pour a small amount into a little plastic container (you can even water it down if you've got an especially delicate job), then use a stiff-bristled artist's brush to smooth it evenly over the surface you want to be sticky. (If you're a stickler about homemade touches, you can also stir up a batch of your own craft glue, using wheat or rice starch and water.)

Glue sticks; lots of cardmakers say they wouldn't do without them, and they're diligent about keeping fresh, clean ones around. Glue sticks glide across the surface of whatever you're gluing, leaving a smooth, even film. Better yet, cleanup involves no more than putting the cap back on. Just keep in mind that the glue from a glue stick dries in a flash. Be sure you're satisfied with the arrangement you're pasting in place. Once it's there, it's there.

Rubber cement is one of those products that has pros and cons when it comes to making cards. Anything you adhere with it is easy to remove, which is convenient if you're re-thinking and rearranging. But, of course, that's also the problem; rubber cement doesn't have perfect staying power. Plus, it tends to yellow over time.

Spray adhesive can't be beat if you want to temporarily position some pieces (the elements of a collage, for example) and make sure you're happy with the layout before gluing them firmly in place. You'll be able to peel

the pieces off, move them around, then fix them in place with craft glue once you've settled on your design. Choose a spray without chlorofluorocarbons, and use it only in a well-ventilated room.

In a different category of adhesive, double-sided tape comes in handy as a sealing device (positioned on the underside of the flap) if you're making your own envelopes. And some cardmakers prefer to use it in place of glue altogether.

Anything Else at All

Seriously. The irresistible allure (and habit-forming fun) of making greeting cards is that nearly anything goes when it comes to the materials that make your cards distinctively *yours*. The designers who've created projects for this book have fastened wire, beads, and lichen (yes, the colorful fungus you find on trees) to their cards. They've fashioned paper-clip people to dance on their cards. And they've covered their cards with everything from buttons and springs to herbs and seeds. One nabbed an empty cement bag when she was in Mexico (she loved the mottled surface), and a strip of it ended up on her Christmas collage card. Another presses her own pansies for focal points on natural-look cards. Paints, candies, mini-gifts, hardware, string, sparkly stickers, the festive-looking foil off the neck of a wine bottle. The point is, anything is fair game for card art.

For some standard techniques, such as stamping and stenciling, you'll need a few additional tools and supplies.

p.s.

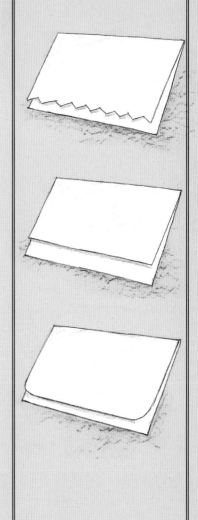

Want your card to have the polished appeal a border can add? An almost instant way to create one is to shorten the front flap of your card and/or alter it in some other way—maybe by trimming the corners or cutting a clever edge on the flap.

GAUGING THE GRAIN

All manufactured papers and most handmade papers have grain, determined by the direction in which a sheet of paper's tiny fibers line up when it's made. Try folding, tearing, or curling a piece of paper with the grain (meaning parallel to it), and you'll have an easy time (and a clean result). Work against the grain, and you're likely to meet resistance (and perhaps end up with a broken or buckled mess). It's especially critical to work parallel with the grain if you're making a card with lots of intricate folds or cuts.

To gauge the grain in a piece of paper, lay it flat and pull one end (the short end, for example) over, resting your hand gently on the curl. Then try the process again, folding the long end over. The paper will look flatter and feel softer when it's folded parallel with the grain. When it's folded against the grain, it will feel stiff and won't fold over as naturally.

We've outlined them in the sections that cover those techniques.

TECHNIQUES

Making a Blank Card

Whether you want a standard blank greeting card, a tiny blank note card, or something in between, the simple process is the same.

■ Decide on the size you want your card to be, and cut a piece of card stock measuring twice the size of one panel of the card you have planned. (For example, if you want your card to be 5 x 7 inches [12.5 x 17.5 cm], cut a piece of card stock 7 x 10 inches [17.5 x 25 cm].) If you're making a card to fit in a purchased envelope, your card should be $^1/_8$ to $^3/_8$ inch (3 mm to 1 cm) smaller than the envelope, depending on the thickness of the card and any additional enclosures.

■ On what will be the inside of your card, mark a line where you want the card to fold with a few light pencil dots, then score the line by running the pointed end of a bone folder along it, using a metal ruler as a guide. This breaks the top fibers in the paper, readying it for a crisp fold.

■ Your card should now easily fold in half along the score line. Sharpen the fold by slowly running the curved edge of the bone folder across it, pressing firmly.

Making an Envelope

If you're making an envelope to fit a specific card, the central rectangle or square of the envelope should be

Cut your card stock

Score the fold line

Sharpen the fold

approximately $^1/_8$ to $^3/_8$ inch (3 mm to 1 cm) larger than the card. We've provided a basic pattern and a couple of alternatives (see page 16). All you do is fold the two side flaps in and the bottom flap up, scoring and sharpening

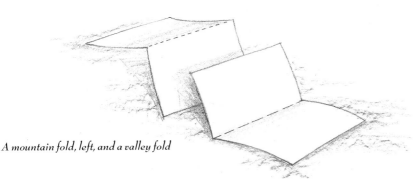

A mountain fold, left, and a valley fold

Printing

There's an endless array of pleasant ways to add pigment and pattern to your cards, from stamping paint in place to pressing it through a mold to simply decorating your cards with hand-printed images. The projects in the Printed Cards chapter incorporate easy approaches. Two of the most popular are stenciling and stamping.

■ Stenciling is simply applying color through a hole (or pattern of holes) cut in a piece of stencil material that is held against the surface you want to decorate. All you need is a stencil (the pattern of cutout holes), color (typically paint), and a tool for applying the color (paintbrushes, stencil brushes, and sponges are most common). You can purchase stencils or make your own. For homemade stencils, choose water-resistant material (such as acetate), and you'll be able to use your stencils over and over.

■ Stamping can become your card-decorating specialty, even if you never set foot in a craft shop. Commercial rubber stamps are now available everywhere from bookstores to airport gift shops. Press them into an ink pad, then on the surface of your card, and you're a stamper. But what's really captivating is creating your own stamps, mostly because the rules are so

satisfyingly loose. If paint or ink will adhere to it, you can create a stamp out of it: fruits, vegetables (potato stamps, of course!), wine corks, sponges, mat board, wood blocks, and—most popular—rubber erasers.

Some materials make interesting stamped impressions just as they are; everything from crumpled tissue paper to dried apple rings. In others, you might want to carve a design. A craft knife works well for most carving jobs. However, if you're working with linoleum blocks (readily available at craft stores), you'll probably want an inexpensive linoleum carving tool and a few interchangeable blades.

Transferring Patterns

For various projects, we've provided patterns you can use to make your own stencils, templates, or stamps.

A photocopy machine is the easiest tool for transferring patterns directly to card stock or to a thin template or stencil material such as acetate (that clear, flimsy plastic used for overhead transparencies). Simply put the card stock or acetate in the copy machine's paper tray and copy the pattern, reducing or enlarging it to meet your needs.

If, instead, you want to transfer a pat-

tern to a thicker material (such as cardboard) to create a sturdy template or to an eraser to create a stamp, you'll need to add a couple of steps. Copy the pattern onto a plain piece of paper first. Then, cut it out, tape it in place on the cardboard or eraser, and trace around it.

p.s.

Keepsake Cards

Hard to believe (especially if a quick glance around your living and working spaces turns up stacks of newspapers, magazines, and printer paper that never seem to go away) but paper doesn't last forever. Its acidity increases with age, meaning it eventually eats into itself and anything touching it (photographs, prints, natural materials, etc.).

Your cards aren't going to disintegrate overnight, but if you want one to be handed down for generations to come, you should create it out of archival paper. Archival paper is neither acidic nor alkaline (pH neutral is what it may say on the packaging), and it should remain chemically stable over time. As extra protection, use an archival adhesive, as well. You should be able to find both in art supply stores.

Mixed Media

NATURAL & FOUND

EVERGREEN WREATH

Designer: Susan L'Hommedieu

This classy little card provides a captivating contrast to the season's tinsel, glitter, and blinking lights. Odds are, when the hustle and bustle die down, it's also the one recipients will remember.

What You Need

Card stock folded into a card or a blank card

Sprigs of fresh evergreen (Flat-needled varieties, such as cedar, work best.)

Raffia or ribbon

Pencil

Drinking glass

Glue

1
Using the bottom of the glass for a pattern, trace a circle in the center of the card.

2
Glue the sprigs of evergreen around the circle until they form a wreath.

3
Tie a tiny bow, and glue it to the bottom of the wreath.

4
Glue one small sprig of evergreen to the flap of the card's envelope.

5
Put the finished card and envelope between the pages of a book to press for a few days. (Evergreens curl and shrink very little as they dry.)

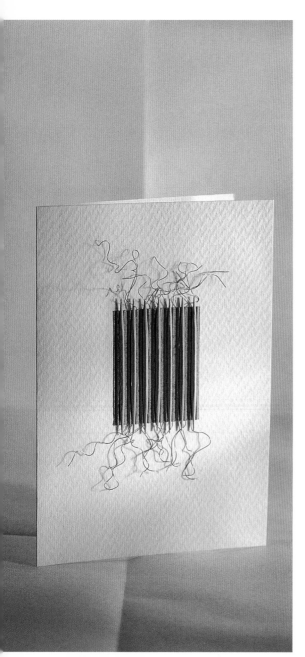

Designer: Terry Taylor

Here's the challenge: Limit yourself to a simple assortment of materials (in this case wire, toothpicks, beads, and a bit more) and see how many collage variations you can construct. Chances are, you'll wind up with a wonderfully clever collection of random acts.

What You Need

Card stock folded into a card or a blank card

Single-face corrugated paper

Toothpicks (round or square; party picks in colors are especially nice)

Selection of embellishments (wire, beads, narrow ribbon, metallic threads, etc.)

Ruler

Pencil

Scissors or craft knife

Glue

Wax paper

Books (for pressing the cards)

1

Cut a piece of corrugated paper 2 x 2¼ inches (5 x 5.6 cm).

2

Glue toothpicks in the grooves of the corrugated paper. You can place one toothpick per groove, skip every other groove, or come up with another pattern. Set the piece aside to dry.

3

Once the corrugated paper and toothpicks are dry, embellish the base piece with some of the other materials. (For example, you can poke short pieces of wire into the grooves of the corrugated paper and curl them around a pencil, string beads across the toothpicks, sew thread through the corrugated paper and leave it dangling in the front, etc.)

4

Glue the corrugated base to a blank card. Cover the base with a scrap of wax paper, and place a book on top to weight it until the design is dry.

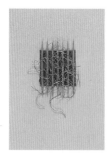

Designer: Susan L'Hommedieu

Hard to imagine better decor for a mailable message than postage stamps. What's more, their variety of shape, size, color, and theme makes them perfect for customizing cards.

What You Need

Card stock folded into a card or a blank card

Canceled stamps

Card stock in 2 different colors (one dark and one light), both of which coordinate with the colors in the stamps

Glue

Pencil

Ruler

Craft knife or scissors

1

Select two stamps that relate to each other in some way, whether they have similar designs (maybe birds, flowers, or flags), complementary colors, or the same theme (perhaps special-issue stamps featuring jazz musicians).

2

With the craft knife, carefully remove any bits of the envelope still stuck around the edges of the stamps.

3

Glue the stamps to the darker color of card stock, then cut them out, leaving a thin, colored border showing around each.

4

Position the stamps on the lighter color piece of card stock (from which you'll cut a piece of backing to frame the bordered stamps). Determine what size you want the backing to be, mark it lightly, and cut it out. (In the project shown, the backing provides a 1/2-inch [1.3 cm] border on the sides and a 3/4-inch [1.9 cm] border at the top and bottom.)

5

Glue the stamps in place on the backing. To lift the stamps away from the card, creating a bit of a three-dimensional look, fold two small pieces of the light-colored card stock until they're each three or four layers thick, then glue the folded pieces between the stamps and the backing, trimming them, if necessary, so they don't show.

6

Glue the backing (with stamps attached) to the center of the card.

Designer: Annie Cicale

Here's an idea that takes personalizing a thank you to a whole new level. Fill a see-through pocket with tokens that represent what you're thankful for—wild flowers gathered on the hike, ticket stubs from the play, a photo snapped at the dinner party. The recipient of the memento-loaded pack will have no doubt that your gratitude is genuine.

What You Need

Card stock folded into a card or a blank card (The front of the card needs to be larger than your largest piece of memorabilia.)

1 piece of decorative paper

1 piece of acetate or another transparent material such as vellum or photocopier transparency film

Mementos of thanks

Glitter and/or confetti

Ruler

Craft knife

Glue

Removable tape

Sewing machine equipped with its smallest needle and fine thread in a color that coordinates with the card

Permanent ink marker

Transfer foil (sold in sheets and rolls at craft stores, available in a variety of colors, and often packaged with the tacky glue you use to apply it)

1

Cut the decorative paper to form a background on the front of the card (leaving a thin border), and glue it in place. Arrange the thank-you mementos you've chosen on top of the paper in a collage fashion, and glue them in place, then sprinkle on the glitter and/or confetti.

2

Cut the acetate or other transparent material to fit the front of the card (leaving a border of approximately $^1/_{16}$ inch [1.5 mm]). Place it on top of the collage, and tack it in place with several pieces of removable tape.

3

Using a decorative stitch on the sewing machine, carefully stitch the acetate to the card, removing each tape piece just before you reach it.

4

Write your message across the front of the card with the marker, then embellish it with transfer foil. Using transfer foil is an easy matter of applying glue in whatever design you choose (swirls, letters, etc.), allowing it to dry thoroughly (overnight is best), then laying the foil over it and rubbing it with your fingers until it transfers. Practice first on a piece of scrap paper. The tip of the glue bottle is one of the best tools for creating a good line with the glue (and some manufacturers sell tips in varying diameters), but you might also experiment with a pen, an artist's brush, or even rubber stamps to get the lines and images you want. When you apply the foil, be sure to press it along the edges of your design, where the glue and paper meet. If you miss a patch, lay a fresh section of foil over the glue, and try again.

Designer: Susan L'Hommedieu

When something ordinary is also artful, it can make your day. If you're a cardmaker, it can also inspire a new design. That's what happened to Susan L'Hommedieu when she spotted these paper clips. The card is clever on its own, but her handwritten punch line inside completes the witty theme. "You've given me so many 'good clips' I thought I should give some to you, too," she wrote. "Thanks for being such a good hairdresser!"

What You Need

Card stock folded into a card or a blank card

Piece of card stock measuring approximately 2 x 3 1/2 inches (5 x 8.8 cm) (This design works best if the color of your card and the smaller piece of card stock repeat the colors in the paper clips.)

Two small scraps of mat board or cardboard

7 colored paper clips that feature a design

Glue

Pen

1

Glue the two small scraps of mat board or cardboard near the center of the back of the piece of card stock.

2

Glue the card stock to the center of the front of the card, using the scraps you attached to the back in step 1 as connection points. This allows the piece of card stock to be raised slightly.

3

Slip the paper clips onto the card stock. You can follow the arrangement shown on this project or come up with your own.

4

Sign your initials under the piece of card stock, if you wish.

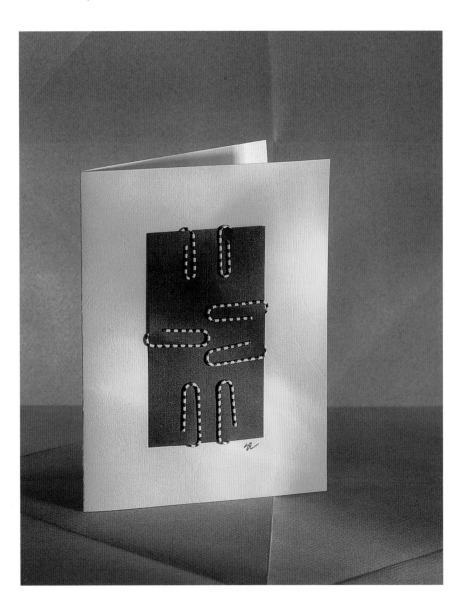

Designer: Linda Anderson

It's easy to transform your handmade message into a full-blown bouquet of greetings.
Simply laminate pressed flowers in place on your card and envelope flap.

What You Need

Card stock folded into a card or a blank card

Pressed flowers and leaves

Sheet of scrap paper

Laminate (available in sheets at craft and office supply stores)

Glue

Artist's brush (unless you're using a glue stick)

Scissors

Deckle scissors (optional)

1

On the sheet of scrap paper, experiment with arrangements of your flowers for the front of your card, layering leaves and random petals underneath and flowers on top, until you're pleased with the design.

2

Coat the surface of your card front with glue, either by rubbing it with a glue stick or brushing on a layer of glue with an artist's brush.

3

Apply the flowers and other materials to the glue-coated surface, pressing them in place gently with the heel of your hand.

4

Cut a piece of laminate that is about 1/4 inch (6 mm) larger than the front of your card. Apply it from the top down, pressing one edge in place, then pulling the laminate across the surface with one hand and smoothing it with the other.

5

Trim the laminate around the card's edges, then rub the surface with the smooth edge of a scissor handle to bring out the color of the flowers underneath.

6

The process of applying flowers and laminate to the flap of your envelope is the same. For added accent, you may want to deckle the edges of the flap. You can do this by hand (see page 16), or use deckle scissors.

7

Store these cards and envelopes in a dark place until you're ready to send them off, otherwise the flowers may fade.

POINTERS ON PRESSING FLOWERS

- Pick flowers for pressing when they're dry (in other words, don't collect them first thing in the morning, when they're still wet with dew, or after a rain).

- Look for small, colorful blossoms (pansies are among the best, since they don't quickly lose their color after being picked), and avoid flowers with fat centers.

- Layer your picks between the pages of a heavy book. (Frequent flower pressers say an old phone book is ideal.)

- Let the pages press the flowers for at least a week, a couple of weeks if possible. If your flowers aren't properly pressed or if they still contain moisture when you incorporate them into a card, they can mildew under the laminate.

If you're going for the botanical specimen look, use a pencil to write the common and Latin name of the flower most prominent in your design along the bottom edge of the front of your card.

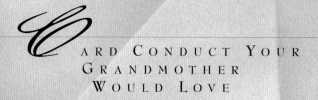

CARD CONDUCT YOUR GRANDMOTHER WOULD LOVE

Tips from times past—when well-mannered correspondence was serious business

From *The New Book of Etiquette*, published by Nelson Doubleday, Inc., 1924

■ The keynote of all good correspondence is simplicity. Flowery language is to be avoided as meticulously as flourishes in handwriting.

■ Odd-shaped envelopes, highly scented notepaper, violent colorings, and gaudy monograms express not individuality, but bad taste.

■ People do not like to receive letters that are crowded with narration of unpleasant things.

■ It is bad taste and poor judgement to write anything of a private or personal nature on a postal card. This type of card, however, may be used to send greetings from a place of interest.

■ People of good taste always use black or dark blue ink for their correspondence. Blots show carelessness, and a fastidious person will rewrite the letter rather than send it with an advertisement of his negligence.

■ The correspondence everyone loves to receive is natural and spontaneous, cheerful in tone, warm with the personality of the writer. It contains news but no gossip.

■ The endings "Very truly yours" or "Yours truly" express a certain formality. More cordial closings are "Yours most sincerely" and "Cordially yours."

YARD ART

Designer: Susan L'Hommedieu

How positively gratifying to create elegant, abstract (and easy!) art out of something everyone else is raking up and bagging. Here, the designer used winged maple seeds—more popularly known as helicopter blades.

What You Need

Card stock folded into a card or a blank card

2 pieces of card stock or decorative paper in coordinating colors (Neutral colors work especially well with natural materials.)

5 winged maple seeds (or other visually appealing seed pods)

Pencil

Ruler

Glue

1

Cut the decorative paper or card stock into two rectangles to be used as a layered background for the center of the card. For the $4^{1}/_{4}$- x $5^{1}/_{2}$-inch (11 x 13.8 cm) card shown, the designer cut a darker piece of card stock measuring 3 x 4 inches (7.5 x 10 cm) and a lighter piece measuring $2^{1}/_{4}$ x 3 inches (5.6 x 7.5 cm).

2

Glue the two rectangles in the center of the card.

3

Glue the winged maple seeds to the layered card stock in an alternating pattern.

4

Using the pencil, write the name of the natural material featured just below the layered card stock, then sign your initials and date the card.

Variations

Two other interesting natural materials that top the designer's list for similar art cards: sweet pea pods and squash seeds.

Designer: Barbara Bussolari

How many hours of television-watching privileges did your mother have to withhold before you finally wrote Aunt Martha to thank her for the socks? Don't be too hard on yourself. Who wouldn't freeze up when faced with blank note paper (and the subject of socks)? If mom had set you up with the makings for a thank-you card like this one, surely you and Aunt Martha would have become pen pals for life.

What You Need

Card stock folded into a card or a blank card

Collection of colorful papers

Yarn

Colored paper clips

Beads and/or buttons

Rouge or lipstick

Scissors

Ruler

Glue

Black marker

Paper edgers

$^1/_8$-inch (3 mm) hole punch

1

From a piece of paper that coordinates with the color of your card, cut two rectangles that measure approximately $^1/_2$ inch (1.3 cm) smaller in perimeter than the folded card. One provides the background for the front of the card; the other (which you may choose to cut from a different color of paper) is for the message inside the card.

2

Center the pieces in place, and glue them down. (If young correspondents are composing the card's message, they may want to write it first before gluing the inside piece down.)

3

Use the black marker to draw a border $^1/_8$ inch (3 mm) out from the background piece. For a more interesting line, use a ruler as a guide, but shake the marker slightly as you draw.

4

Use paper edgers to cut a head (a circle), a body (an off-set rectangle), and feet and hands (random small shapes) out of various colors of paper. The less perfect these pieces are, the more enchanting.

5

With the hole punch, make holes for paper-clip limbs in the four corners of the rectangle and at the ends of the feet and hands. Punch holes along the top of the head for attaching hair.

6

For hair, tie or loop a strand of yarn through each of the holes, and trim it to the length you want.

7

Draw on eyes and a mouth, adding a bit of "blush" to the cheeks with your finger.

8

Attach the feet and hands to the body with various colors of paper clips, and glue on some buttons and/or beads.

9

Glue the head to the body. Once it's dry, glue the head to the card. It holds the body in place while allowing it to stick out and frolic a bit on the front.

Variations

■ Use brads to connect the body parts, or tie them together with yarn.

■ Adapt patterns for other figures from coloring books.

Designer: Helen Robinson

These industrial-strength cards have the look of an inner-city factory turned artist's loft. Raid the nearest construction site or warehouse demolition (or simply head to the hardware store) to collect raw materials for your own.

What You Need

Card stock folded into a card or a blank card (choose muted, cool colors)

Several sheets of texturized watercolor paper

Oil painting sticks

Colored pencils

Random hardware, such as springs, washers, sheets of thin, galvanized steel (cut-up tin cans work well, too), anodized aluminum rods (typically sold in thin rods measuring approximately 12 inches [30 cm] long), etc.

Random craft supplies, such as spools of colored wire, tubular glass beads, round beads, etc.

Sturdy wire (such as 20-gauge beading wire)

Glue

Sturdy scissors

Metal cutting shears (available at hardware stores; optional)

Metal hole punch (available at hardware stores; optional)

Hole punch

1

With the oil painting sticks and colored pencils, create an abstract design on watercolor paper, then cut the design into random shapes. For some variations of this card, you'll want to use a colored shape as part of the collage. Simply glue the shape to the front of the card, wrapping its ends over and gluing them to the inside front cover of the card or to the back of the card, if you like. (As an alternative to creating your own design, you can use wallpaper samples, wrapping paper, or photographs from art magazines.)

2

Create a collage of hardware and craft materials to hang from or attach to your card. For some variations, you may want to combine the collage of materials with the painted shape; for others, you may want the collage of materials to stand alone.

✳ For the card pictured on the facing page, the designer threaded tiny gold beads onto thin red and gold craft wire, then scrunched a handful of the beaded wire into a flat, rounded shape. She used scissors to cut a 3-inch (7.5 cm) section of an anodized aluminum rod, threaded a sturdier piece of wire through the rod, attached one end of the sturdier wire to the colored-wire creation, and hooked the other through a hole she punched near the top of the card. She finished the design by adding a smudge of color behind the hanging collage with a gold oil painting stick.

✳ For the card pictured above, the designer cut a moon from textured watercolor paper she had painted with a silver oil painting stick. She punched holes in the moon with a hole punch, then attached light emitting diodes (sold in electronics stores as indicator

lights for electronic equipment) and washers, holding the washers in place first, then sticking the two tiny wires that protrude from the lights through

the holes. She hung the collage by threading the wires through holes punched in the card and bending them to hold the collage in place.

Variations

■ Use sturdy wire to attach interesting beads and various colors of aluminum rod sections to your cards (below left); use metal cutting shears to cut galvanized steel or tin from tin cans into various shapes, punch them with holes using a metal punch, and attach beads and coiled wire through the holes (below center); string tubular glass beads on colored wire and attach the beaded wire through a hole punched in the card, shade your steel or tin with an oil painting stick, and attach a magnet to the metal (below right).

Do your friends and family back home really need another seen-one-seen-'em-all shot of a vacation-spot skyline? Traveling puts loads of raw material at your fingertips (think local sand, ticket stubs, playbills). Every bit of it can be used to piece together one-of-a-kind travel reports. Here are three takes on ways to personalize yours.

TRAVELOGUE
TAKE 1

Designer: Barbara Bussolari

What You Need

Card stock folded into a card or a blank card

Collection of colored paper

Mementos from a trip, such as maps, flyers, small shells, etc.

Purchased stickers that match your theme (In this project, the designer used a crab and a turtle to help decorate a card about a trip to Disney World.)

Ruler

Scissors or craft knife

Glue

Black marker

1

From a piece of paper that coordinates with the color of your postcard or card, cut a rectangle that measures approximately ¹/₂ inch (1.3 cm) smaller in perimeter than the postcard or folded card, and glue it to the front of the card.

2

Use the black marker to draw a border ¹/₈ inch (3 mm) out from the rectangular piece. For a more interesting line, use a ruler as a guide, but shake the marker slightly as you draw.

3

Cut or tear out pieces from maps or brochures to serve as a layered background for your card, playing with the layout. Once you're pleased with the design, glue the pieces in place and add the stickers.

4

Add heavier objects (such as the shells and sand on the project shown) last, settling them in a thick layer of strong glue.

Variations

■ Make color copies of photos from your trip (or run the photos through a scanner), and include these images in your personalized collage.

■ If you're making a card that needs an envelope, create your own out of a map from the area you visited.

Designer: Brigid Burns

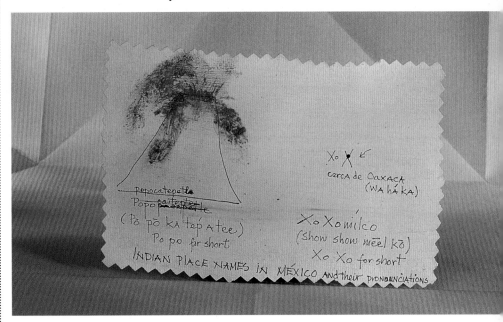

What You Need

Purchased blank postcards or handmade blank postcards, measuring 4 x 6 inches (10 x 15 cm), cut from stiff drawing paper

Gesso (optional) (You can use this primer to texturize the surface of your postcards. If you plan to use oil paints in your design, the gesso will prevent them from running.)

Drawing and decorating materials (colored pencils, paints, pens, etc.)

Local inspiration (What sets these postcards apart is that they're made "on the scene," with local materials and subject matter providing the muse.)

Pinking shears

Paintbrush (optional)

Glue (optional)

1

Prep your postcards before leaving home by coating them with gesso, if you like, and (to add a bit of personalized vintage appeal) trimming the edges with pinking shears.

2

Pack your pre-treated postcards and drawing and gluing supplies.

3

Once you're settled somewhere, whether it's a hotel room, a safari tent, or a cabin at a base camp, set up your traveling studio (that is, unpack the postcards and drawing and gluing supplies).

4

Relax and wait for the creativity that inevitably accompanies time away to bubble up. Keep your eyes peeled for materials and messages that will personalize your cards. It helps to think of these cards as journal entries rather than finished pieces of art. During a long stay in San Miguel de Allende, Mexico, the designer created the card shown as part of a series. She sketched a simple volcano with a pencil, glued on some cement mix she found in the street to represent volcano ash, and drew flames with a colored pencil. With ink, she added Indian words and place names (complete with phonetic pronunciations). She also decided that cross-outs and changes made the one-of-a-kind card all the more enchanting.

Designer: D a n a   I r w i n

What You Need

Card stock folded into a card or a blank card

Local landmark from which to create a rubbing (The design shown features a city water main lid from Granada, Spain.)

Flexible paper (medium-to-light in weight)

1 piece of thin cardboard or mat board

Tape

Colored pencil, crayon, charcoal, or rubbing wax

Access to a photocopy machine (color or black and white)

Access to a scanner, a computer equipped with software that allows you to manipulate scanned photographs, and a color printer (optional) (A full-service photocopy shop with customer work stations should provide you with access to all this equipment.)

No. 2 pencil or soft art pencil

Ruler

Craft knife

Glue

1

Make a rubbing of any raised or engraved surface you happen upon in your travels. (Historic markers, tombstones, and street signs all make great images.) Simply place your paper over the surface, taping it in place if necessary, and lightly rub your writing instrument across the paper in controlled strokes until the image appears. (The more controlled your strokes, the more even your rubbed image.)

2

On the front of the card, use the pencil to lightly mark a window opening $1/8$ inch (3 mm) larger than the size you have planned for your finished design.

3

Open the card up flat, and use a very sharp craft knife to cut out the opening, working from the front. Use a ruler to make your cuts as straight as possible, placing the ruler so you are cutting between it and the piece that will be removed. That way, if the knife slips slightly while cutting, you won't damage the face of the card.

4

For a low-tech version of this card, make a black-and-white or color photocopy of your rubbing, reducing or enlarging it to fit the window opening you cut. If you want to incorporate more technology, scan the rubbing as a black-and-white image. Then, using a computer design program, assign a color to the image, and manipulate the design, if you wish. You can use separate pieces of the image to create a bor-

der, reposition elements of the image to create your own composition, etc. Print out your design on a color printer.

5

Mark a border that leaves a $1/2$-inch (1.3 cm) frame of paper around your image and cut the image out along the border.

6

Run a bead of glue along the edge of the cut-out image and glue it to the inside of the card's front panel, so it shows through the opening. To add to the antique look, make light marks with a No. 2 pencil or soft art pencil around the window opening on the front of the card and smudge them with your fingers to pick up the texture of the paper.

7

Cut the cardboard or mat board to a size slightly smaller than your folded card, and glue it to the inside front cover.

Variation
....

Mixed Media

PAPER & FABRIC

Designer: Pei-Ling Becker

Add some ancient wisdom to your next handmade birthday card. If you've eaten at a Chinese restaurant, you know the Chinese zodiac system, spelled out in brilliant red and gold on the standard-issue place mats. Clip the animal-year combination that fits, and use it as a focal point for an exquisite birthday collage.

What You Need

Card stock folded into a card or a blank card

Place mat from a Chinese restaurant

Variety of decorative paper

Miscellaneous supplies for embellishing the paper (glitter, metallic pens, etc.) (optional)

Miscellaneous small trinkets and found objects (beads, buttons, etc.)

Small square of foam core (optional)

Needle and thread for attaching various found objects (optional)

Craft knife (optional)

Glue

1
Cut or tear the zodiac illustration and description you've chosen from the place mat. (If you like, use a photocopy machine to enlarge the image—and make it black and white—first.)

2
Cut and/or tear the decorative paper into various shapes. You may want to decorate some of the scraps using simple techniques such as gluing on glitter.

3
Arrange and layer the paper on the front of the card until you're pleased with the design. Glue it in place.

4
Add any trinkets or found objects you want to include, sewing or gluing them in place, as necessary.

5
Add the zodiac illustration and description to your design. (If you want this image raised slightly, mount it on a backing of thin foam core before gluing it to the card.)

Variation

Designer: Susan L'Hommedieu

The most you've got to master to make a card like this is the pleasing scrunching and crinkling action necessary to mold the paper heart. Combine it with the snazzy color combination of black and gold, and the effect is elegant as can be.

What You Need

Black card stock folded into a card

Red tissue (If you can find some printed with gold designs like the stars on the paper in this project, your card will glisten.)

Metallic gold cardboard

Ruler

Craft knife or scissors

Glue

Metallic gold pen

1

Cut the gold cardboard so that it will fit on the face of the card while leaving a border of approximately ¹/₂ inch (1.3 cm) on the sides and 1¹/₄ inches (3.1 cm) on the top and bottom.

2

Center the gold cardboard, and glue it in place.

3

Cut a piece of tissue paper about 1 inch (2.5 cm) larger in length and width than the card face.

4

Lay the tissue face up on the assembled card, and begin to turn the edges under as you scrunch and crinkle the tissue paper into the shape of a heart. Allow imperfection—and no excessive scrunching! By working on top of the card, you'll be able to scrunch together a heart that is the appropriate size.

5

Using only tiny spots of glue (to avoid saturating the thin paper), glue the heart in place over the gold cardboard.

6

Sign your initials with the metallic gold pen, if you like, and use the pen to write your message inside.

Paint Chip Bamboo

Designer: Lisa Sanders

With labels as irresistible as "tiger lily," "limón," and "dahlia mauve," it makes perfect sense that those fabulous strips and chips of color you collect when shopping for paint would make a spectacular collage on a card. Designer Lisa Sanders saw the gradations of green on one set of strips as stalks of tropical grass.

What You Need

Card stock folded into a card or a blank card or postcard

Strips of green color swatches from a paint store

Craft knife

Ruler

Pencil

Glue

Artist's brush

1

With the ruler and pencil, draw a line along the longer edge of the swatch card, and use it as a guide to trim off any color names and numbers. (You may need to trim both edges.)

2

Divide what remains of the swatch card into six sections ranging from ¹/₈ inch (3 mm) to ¹/₄ inch (6 mm) wide and running the length of the swatch card.

3

Using the ruler as a guide, cut out the six sections.

4

Place the sections, running horizontally and slanted with uneven spacing, on the card, keeping the darker shades all at the same end.

Designer: Margaret Desmond Dahm

It's so much simpler than pressing stone or tile into mortar.
But this paper mosaic is an intricate work of art nonetheless.

What You Need

Card stock folded into a card or a
blank card (Remember when choosing
your card color that the card surface will
serve as the "grout" in your mosaic.)

Blank sheet of paper

Sheets torn from magazines featuring
various colors and patterns (You may
also want to add touches of other
materials, such as the aluminum foil
bubbles in the project shown.)

Pencil

Craft knife or scissors

Glue in a squeeze container

1

Sketch your design on the blank sheet
of paper, referring to patterns, pieces
of clip art, or images from books or
magazines as guides, if you like.
Lightly transfer the design to the
front of your card (see Transferring
Patterns, page 19).

2

Based on your design, choose colors for
your mosaic pieces (which are called
tesserae by those who do this regu-
larly). In the project shown, the
designer chose yellow and red for the
fish, orange for the fins, and various
shades of blue for the water. Use a
craft knife or scissors to cut your colors of choice from magazine pictures,

cutting small, squarish shapes measuring approximately ¹/₄ inch (6 mm)
square. (Helpful hint: This takes
awhile. It's a good step to pair with a
video tape you've been dying to watch
or a new CD you haven't yet had a
chance to crank up.) As you work, try
to keep your pieces grouped by color.

3

Run a bead of glue along a short
stretch of one of the lines of your
design, and begin evenly laying down
tesserae, remembering to leave bits of
space in between each piece so the
"grout" shows. Continue laying down
pieces in any order that makes sense
(outlining first and then filling in, or
working from one end of a feature—say
the fish's head—to the other). Try to
lay the pieces in a way that reflects the
contours of the object you're depicting
(using rounded rows on a ball, for
example, wavy lines in water, or
straight lines on a building). As you
work, you'll likely need to trim, cut
squares into triangles, round some corners, etc., to make the tesserae fit your
design.

4

When your design is completely filled
in, dab away any glue that is seeping
out. (The good news is that this is a for-
giving medium; any excess glue will
dry clear.) Cover the card with a piece
of paper, and place it under a heavy
book to dry.

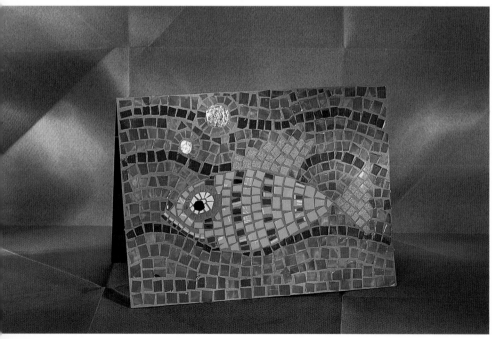

Designer: Kate Harper

Wait! If the word painted in this project's title makes you want to turn the page ("I'm not a painter; give me a cutting-and-pasting project."), here's your chance to surprise yourself. If you can doodle, you can do this.

What You Need

Card stock folded into a card or a blank card

Mat board scraps (Check the trash can near the paper cutter at the nearest framing shop or art supply store.)

Acrylic medium (a clear varnish available at art and craft stores)

Variety of non-water-based paint markers

Colored corrugated cardboard

Artist's brush

Scissors

Glue

1
Use the artist's brush to coat your mat board scraps with the acrylic medium, and let them dry.

2
With the paint pens, decorate the scraps with simple designs, patterns, and words. (Dots, squiggles, and swirls are ideal.)

3
Cut the mat board into random, interesting shapes.

4
Arrange the mat board shapes on a piece of corrugated cardboard, then cut the cardboard to a size that provides a good background for the arrangement.

5
Glue the cardboard to the front of the card and the mat board to the cardboard.

6
Place a weight (a book is just the thing) on top of the card, and let it dry for at least an hour.

Variations

Designer: Brigid Burns

This celebration in sound bites is the quintessential computer-age card. Fire up the technological tools (or grab a stack of magazines), and set about splicing together your own mix of verbal and visual wit.

What You Need

Any means of getting words onto a piece of paper (see step 1)

Plain paper, trimmed to desired size, to print or paste words upon (In the design shown, the paper measures 4³/₄ x 6³/₄ inches [12 x 16.9 cm].)

Scrap of decorative paper

Scissors or craft knife

Artist's brush

Glue

Access to a photocopy machine

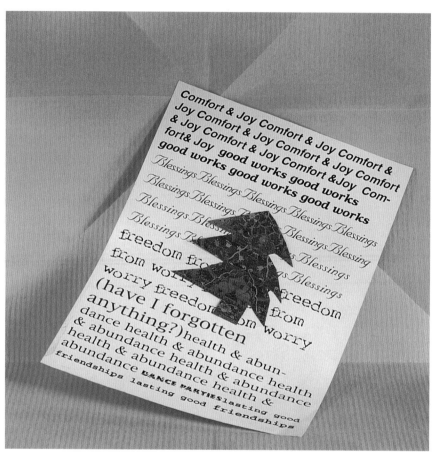

1

Play with putting words on a page to communicate your message, experimenting with the interplay of various sizes and styles of type. Changing the graphic elements to suit each new phrase can create the effect of different "voices." A computer with a basic word processing program allows you to play with typefaces, sizes, and placements; all you need is a printer to print them out. A desktop publishing program offers more elaborate design options, and a color printer allows you to print your words in shades other than black. For a low-tech approach that achieves a similar effect, search magazines and newspapers for interesting typefaces and copy. Clip what you like, and experiment with laying out the clips as a running collage.

2

Once you've settled on your collage of words and phrases, print it out. (If you clipped your words and phrases, brush the backs of the clips with glue and press them in place.)

3

From the decorative paper, cut a single image that is in keeping with your theme, and glue it in place on top of your collage.

4

For a finished look—and for producing mass quantities of your card—copy the collage of words and images onto card stock, using either a black-and-white or a color copier.

Designer: Margaret Desmond Dahm

If you want your message to pack the punch of age-old knowledge (not to mention conjure images of scribes scribbling by the banks of the Nile), craft your card out of this important-looking paper.

What You Need

Thick white paper

Strong coffee or tea

Iron and a flat surface to iron on (A countertop covered with a towel works well.)

Old toothbrush

Craft knife

Matches

Long candle

1

Lay the sheet of paper on the flat surface, and pour a tablespoon or so of the coffee or tea onto the paper, tipping the edges of the paper so that the liquid coats the surface. Let the paper sit for one minute, then swish the liquid around some more. Repeat this process until the surface is a mottled brown.

2

While the paper is still wet, iron it flat with a medium-to-hot iron. Be sure the steam setting on the iron is off, since you're attempting to remove moisture from the paper.

3

If you want more of a mottled effect, douse the toothbrush in the coffee or tea, then run your thumb over the bristles to sprinkle the liquid on the paper. Run the iron over the paper again once you're pleased with the splatters of discoloration.

4

When the paper is completely dry, cut out the approximate shape you want. If you plan to roll your greeting up as a scroll, you may not cut the paper at all. For other variations, you might cut a piece to be pasted on the front of a blank card, or an even smaller piece to back the first letter in a handwritten note.

5

Take the paper outside. Steering clear of any other flammable objects, light the candle, and with the paper in one hand and the burning candle in the other, touch the flame to a small area of the paper. Let it just begin to burn, then blow out the flame. Work slowly, singeing the paper all the way around. A few safety suggestions: It's critical that you light only small areas of paper at a time. Also, since paper is good at burning, it may keep doing so even after you think you've blown out the flame completely; be sure to check each section carefully as you finish with it to make sure nothing is still smoldering.

6

After the paper is cool, gently break off the dark, burnt pieces, leaving an "aged" edge.

Designer: Kerry Harvey-Piper

A card that requires you to eat three pieces of candy before you can make it? What are you waiting for?

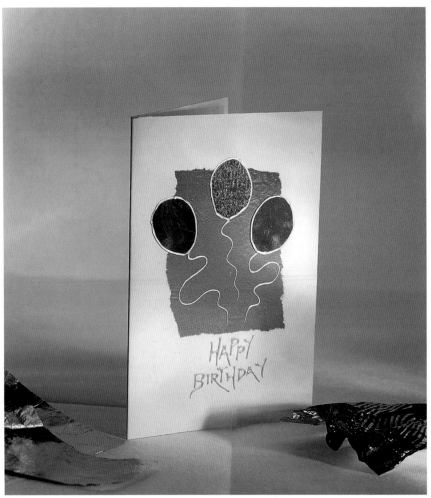

What You Need

Card stock folded into a card or a blank card

Colored tissue paper or crepe paper for the sky; rainbow-colored paper is great, or wrapping paper with clouds printed on it

3 different-colored scraps of bright, shiny paper; candy wrappers are ideal

Tube of gold or silver glitter glue

Tube of gold fabric paint

Pencil

Ruler

Scissors or craft knife

Glue

Small artist's brush

1

Mark a rectangle on the tissue paper, approximately half the width and two-thirds the length of the front of your card. Cut it out with the scissors or a craft knife, or, for a softer look, tear it out. Paint the back with glue, and paste it to the front of your card.

2

Draw balloon shapes on each of the candy wrappers, and carefully cut them out.

3

Glue the balloons over the tissue-paper sky. Positioning one slightly higher than the other two lends some perspective to the design.

4

When the glue is dry, use the glitter glue to outline the balloons (giving them a smoother, more finished look) and paint on the strings. The lines should be wavy, to give a sense of movement.

5

For a special occasion such as a birthday, use the fabric paint to write your message underneath the picture.

FABRIC, STITCH & STAMP

Designer: Sandy Webster

These evocative cards mix imagery and materials to carry out themes. One features gingham cloth, flower stamps, and clips of summertime scenes. Another showcases a wood-block Christmas tree print with stitched-on branches. Whatever approach you take, the charm is in the mingling.

What You Need

Card stock folded into a card or a blank card

Purchased stamps or your own stamps carved from linoleum, wood, or erasers (For details on transferring an image to stamp material and carving it, see page 72.)

Stamp pads

Printed imagery related to celebratory occasions (Old books and pieces of gift wrap are two good sources.)

Fabric scraps

Thread

Small sticks and other found objects

Decorative papers you can stitch through

Small scraps of mat board (optional)

Scissors

Glue

Needle

1

Play with collage combinations, picking and choosing from the materials you've assembled, until you come up with one you like (narrowing your final choice, perhaps, to a stamp, an image, and some fabric).

2

Cut a piece of decorative paper to fit on the front of your card. There are no hard-and-fast rules on this; simply cut it to a size that suits you, using the photos shown here for ideas. (You may even decide to layer several pieces of paper, or combine paper and fabric.)

3

Stamp your image(s) on the paper, then assemble your other collage materials. Glue some in place; sew others, playing with both delicate and bold stitches. For added texture, you may want to stamp small images on tiny scraps of mat board and add them to the collage.

4

If you like, stitch a loose border around your collage, and leave the ends of the thread dangling in front.

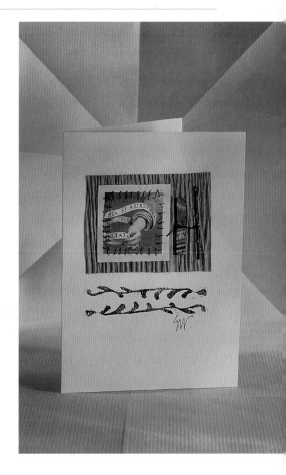

Variations

Designer: Allison Stilwell

If you've got a passing acquaintance with a sewing machine and can use it to stitch a somewhat straight seam, you'll have no problem tailoring one of these utterly heartwarming cards.

What You Need

Card stock folded into a card or a blank card

Fabric scraps

6-inch (15 cm) square of fabric

Handful of seed beads (tiny glass beads named for the kernels they resemble)

Metallic gold thread

Thread that coordinates with your fabric scraps

Straight pins

Sewing machine (with the bobbin filled with thread to coordinate with your fabric scraps)

Scissors

Thin beading needle

Metallic gel marker

Heart stamp

Stamping ink

Red colored pencil

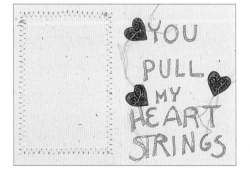

Inside view

1

Cut the fabric scraps into small pieces, then use them to form a collage on the 6-inch (15 cm) square of fabric. Once you're pleased with the collage, attach the scraps to the fabric square with straight pins.

2

With the sewing machine, carefully stitch around the pins enough to tack the scraps in place, then remove the pins and sew freely all over the fabric scraps until you like the look.

3

Cut a heart out of the fabric collage, and decorate it by sewing on a selection of seed beads with the beading needle and coordinating thread.

4

Set your sewing machine for a large zigzag stitch, and slowly stitch a border around your card. (A card with an embossed edge around it gives you a nice line to follow. If your card doesn't have one, lightly mark a border to sew over.)

5

Thread the needle with metallic thread, and attach the heart to the front of the card with three tacking stitches, using a doubled thread that you haven't knotted. Hold the heart on the front of the card, and insert the needle from the front of the heart through the heart and card, leaving a

2-inch (5 cm) tail on the front. Move your needle over about ⅛ inch (3 mm), and come back up through the card and the heart. Tie a knot using the tail and the longer piece of thread, and clip the ends, leaving some straggles of dangling thread. Repeat this process at least two more times to securely attach the heart to the card.

6

With the metallic gel marker, write "You pull my heartstrings" on the inside of the card. Stamp hearts around the message, and color them in with the pencil. Add some stitches inside, using the same technique you used to attach the heart to the card.

p.s.

a tiny stamped heart with its own heartstrings on the envelope flap helps finish the look of your package.

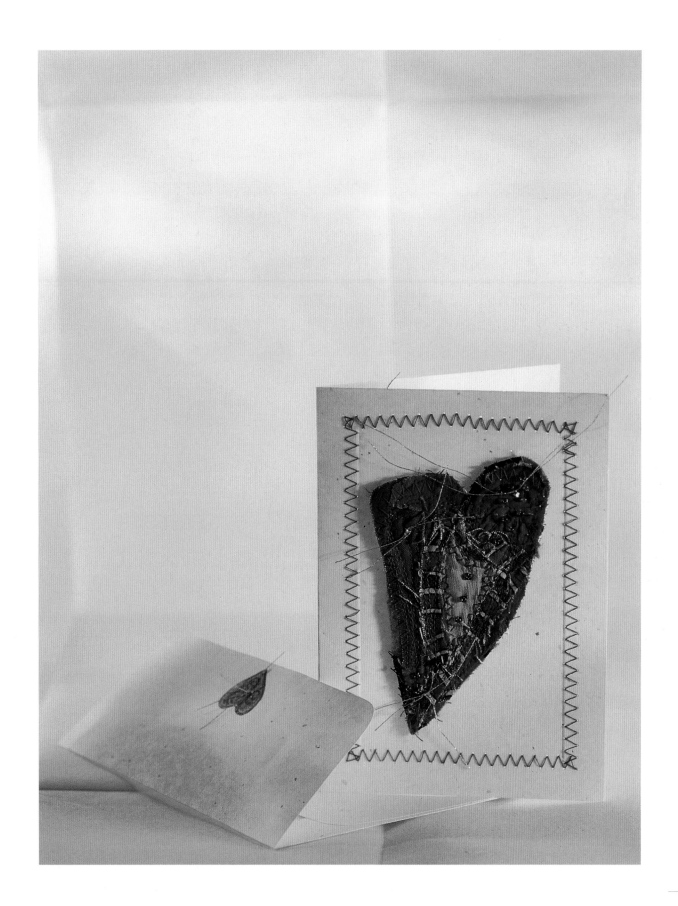

𝒯HE POSTCARD PROPOSAL

My girlfriend of several years, Hannah Harris, and I had talked about marriage at length months before I took a trip to represent my company, John Neal, Bookseller, at an international calligraphy conference at the University of San Diego. But with our busy schedules, we had "gotten on with our lives," and the issue of marriage faded. Once at the conference, I decided I was ready to put into action a proposal idea I had thought of some time back.

I bought 15 blank postcards, then asked 15 of the conference's world-renowned instructors to each write one letter or symbol on a card: W, I, L, L, Y, O, U, M, A, R, R, Y, M, E—and a question mark. They were happy to participate.

I mailed the postcards to Hannah from San Diego as I got them back from the artists, so they did not reach her in any particular order. It didn't take her long to catch on to what was happening, but I refused to talk about it until the question was complete.

I had time to get home and get an engagement ring before the last postcard arrived. After it did, we went for a walk on the farm where we live. Down by the creek, in a field of flowers, I pulled out the ring and officially asked Hannah to marry me. She said yes. We were married the following spring and honeymooned in the fall in Scotland.

Kenneth Mansfield

Please see Contributing Designers, page 125, for the names of the artists who created each postcard.

THE GUARDIAN

Designer: Pei-Ling Becker

This fabric-focused assemblage features a scrap from an old shirt decorated with a traditional Indonesian pattern known as The Guardian. Create your own variation by recycling any textile design that catches your eye.

What You Need

Card stock folded into a card or a blank card

Piece of handmade paper that is smaller than the front of your card

Piece of old fabric with an interesting pattern, cut to fit atop the handmade paper

Bright beads

Tree twig or other found object

Thread and needle

Glue

Artist's brush

1

Using the artist's brush, glue the fabric to the handmade paper.

2

Decorate the piece by sewing beads in random patterns (stringing some together, if you like) to the fabric and gluing a found object or two to the fabric or paper.

3

Glue the decorated piece to the front of the card.

Designer: Tracy Page Stilwell

The designer used a computer program to create this funky collage featuring a message-eating fish.

You can manipulate images on a screen to come up with your own collage pieces, or simply clip some from printed sources.

What You Need

Collage piece for the front of the card measuring approximately 4 x 5 inches (10 x 12.5 cm) (You have lots of options: print a computer-generated collage out on a black-and-white or color printer; cut and paste a collage and use it as is; or cut and paste a collage, then create a smooth piece by running it through a black-and-white or color copier.)

Image to wrap around half of your card (Choose your image based on the theme of the collage on the front.)

Colored card stock measuring 6 x 12 inches (15 x 30 cm)

Ruler

Bone folder

Glue

Marker

1

Looking at the card stock lengthwise, make a mark 2 1/2 inches (6.25 cm) in from the right and 4 1/2 inches (11.3 cm) in from the left. Fold the card stock in at each mark (folding the right-hand fold first) and crease both folds with the bone folder.

2

Glue the 4 x 5-inch (10 x 12.5 cm) collage piece to the front of the card (which you created with the second fold in step 1).

3

Glue the second image so it wraps from the back of the card around the shorter flap and extends past the edge.

4

Add a message to the inside with the marker, allowing the message to interact with the wrap-around-image, if possible.

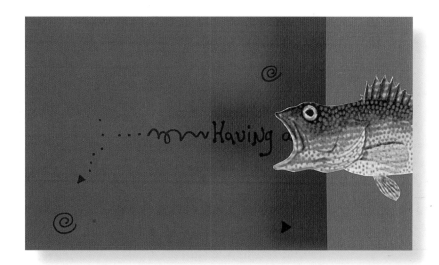

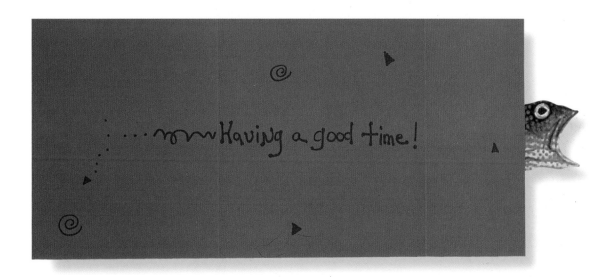

Printed

CARDS

Designer: Kate Harper

A single, simple stamp can create a stunningly elegant card. Homemade rubber stamps cut out of the humble erasers we all remember from school days have a pleasingly rough texture—and imperfections that are their charm.

What You Need

Card stock folded into a card or a blank card

Gum eraser

Multicolored ink pad

Black marker

Craft knife

Pencil

1

Draw a simple image onto the eraser with the marker. (In the project shown, the designer drew a package with a bow on top.)

2

Cut out the image with the craft knife.

3

Coat the stamp with ink by pressing it into the ink pad, then stamp the card.

4

Add some artistic flair by signing your initials in pencil under the image.

P.S.

Don't always be tempted to fill the space on the front of your card with lots of images. Sometimes the smallest, sparest image is the most stunning.

Designer: Mardi Dover Letson

Whether you're sending congratulations to transplanted friends or updating others on your own relocation, this charming communiqué captures the home-sweet-home spirit.

What You Need

Card stock folded into a card or a blank card

Decorative paper and card stock in several complementary colors

Ink pad (Choose a color of ink that coordinates with your paper choices.)

Purchased button with a house theme

Raffia

Set of commercial or handmade alphabet stamps

Craft knife or paper cutter

Glue

$^1/_8$-inch (3 mm) hole punch

1

Stamp individual letters to spell "New Home" (or whatever message you choose) onto one of your pieces of decorative paper or card stock. Use the craft knife or paper cutter to cut the letters out into block shapes.

2

Glue the stamped blocks onto a second color of paper, spreading the glue evenly to the edges of each block before attaching it. Cut the new layered blocks out, leaving a colored frame of approximately $^1/_{16}$ inch (1.5 mm).

3

Repeat the framing process once more, using a third color of paper, so that you end up with stamped blocks layered on top of two color-coordinated blocks.

4

Experiment with positioning the stamped blocks and the button on the card until you're pleased with the arrangement, then glue the blocks in place.

5

To attach the button, punch two holes where you want it, thread the raffia through the button and the holes, and tie it off with a neat knot inside.

Designer: Allison Stilwell and four-year-old grandson Gabriel

This endearing card is printing at its simplest—and sweetest: a child's colored pencil drawing. The designer set out to have her grandson help make a Mother's Day card for her mother. The artistic approach was a time-honored one: sitting together, talking, and drawing pictures. When her grandson came up with a rendering of his own mother picking flowers, the designer knew she had a one-of-a-kind family card. Here's how to create your own.

What You Need

Oil colored pencils

Several sheets of card stock

Handmade paper that matches or contrasts nicely with your card stock

Glue

Paper edgers

Ruler

Scissors or craft knife

Press type (optional) (Available at office supply and craft stores, the sizes and shapes of press type vary. If you're not fond of your own hand writing, press type provides a way to rub on one pre-formed letter at a time.)

1

Have a young family member make a drawing. Typically, there's no further instruction necessary; kids have great artistic instinct.

2

Trim the paper in a way that frames the drawing well. Glue it to a sheet of handmade paper, then use the edgers to make a fun border out of the paper.

3

Cut a piece of card stock to match the size of the bordered drawing, with an added ¹/₂ inch (1.3 cm) on the left edge.

4

Fold that extra ¹/₂ inch (1.3 cm) over, coat the outside of the folded-over strip with glue, and attach it to the back of the drawing.

5

Use press type or hand lettering to add a message.

Inside view

Designer: Margaret Desmond Dahm

Add a food quote to one, enclose a favorite recipe in another, tuck a third in a gift basket of goodies, send a fourth as a dinner-party thank you. With their smorgasbord of uses, these colorful cards featuring food are a treat to have on hand.

What You Need

Card stock folded into a card or a blank card

Stencil material (acetate or heavy card stock)

Acrylic paint

Piece of scrap paper

Masking tape

Craft knife

Cutting board or other cutting surface (sheet of corrugated cardboard, telephone book, or magazine)

Large plastic lid to serve as a paint palette (The top of a large yogurt container works well.)

Sponge (Any kind, from a standard kitchen sponge to a cosmetic sponge, will do.)

Ruler

Colored pencils

1

Transfer one of the patterns from page 59 to the stencil material.

2

With a craft knife, carefully cut out the pattern, one small section at a time. If you make a cut that isn't complete (say it leaves part of a section you're trying to remove in place), don't pull on the remaining piece and risk damaging the stencil; re-cut the section. When you're finished, you can remove the pattern and hold the stencil up to get an idea of what it will look like when it's printed.

3

Pour some acrylic paint into the upturned plastic lid. Add a bit of water, if necessary, until the paint is the consistency of sour cream.

4

Before using the stencil to apply ink to your card, try a sample design on a sheet of scrap paper. Dip a corner of the sponge into the paint, hold the stencil flat on the paper, and dab at the openings with paint until you've covered all of them. Lift the stencil straight up, and review the design. Experiment with more or less ink and more or less pressure until you achieve a look you're happy with.

5

When you're ready to use the stencil on a card, tape the card to a flat surface, place the stencil on the card according to where you want the design to appear (using a ruler to position it, if necessary), and tape it in place with a piece of tape at each corner. (Here's a trick for treating your tape so it's still sticky but won't tear your stencil or card when you remove it: Stick the tape to a clean piece of fabric, and pull it back off before using it.)

6

Starting at one end of the stencil and moving to the other, dab your paint onto the openings. After you've covered them all, pull up one taped end of the stencil, lifting it as you remove the tape, then pull up the other end and carefully lift the stencil off completely.

7

After the design is dry, use a variety of colored pencils to shade it in. Pencils that provide a more opaque look allow you to color in layers and achieve an almost painted effect.

Here are some notes on the colors the designer used on the cards shown.

*❋ **Coffee cup:*** With pencils almost the colors of the cards themselves, she shaded the steam in very lightly.

*❋ **Country loaf:*** She used a cream-colored pencil for the cut marks on top of the loaf, and colored the loaf itself with two shades of brown, the darker on the bottom of the loaf and the lighter on top.

*❋ **Garlic:*** On one side of each clove she shaded in white accents; she used dark accents on the other side.

Stencil patterns, top to bottom: garlic, coffee cup, chile peppers, country loaf

* **Chile peppers:** After stenciling the design on the card, the designer used a ruler to draw a checkerboard grid on the rest of the card, then used two different strokes (one diagonal and one up and down), which she alternated from square to square in colors similar to the card-stock color. She colored the peppers red and accented them with green.

Variations

....

Designer: Kate Harper

Got a large group of eager young hands and a limited cardmaking budget? Let your budding artists stamp away. They'll be delighted with the abstract card art they can create, using the humblest of materials and the simplest of techniques.

What You Need

Card stock folded into a card or a blank card

Construction paper in an assortment of colors, measuring at least 14 x 17 inches (35 x 42.5 cm) (1 piece per child) (High-quality, non-crumbling construction paper works best. Or, for a real low-cost but striking option, use paper bags.)

Sponges cut into halves or fourths

Gum or rubber erasers with flat, rectangular sides

Plastic tubs (Margarine tubs are perfect.)

Non-toxic, water-based paint, slightly diluted

Found objects, such as cardboard and twine

Scissors

Glue

1
Pour approximately ¼ cup (60 mL) of paint into each plastic tub (pouring a different color into each tub), and put an eraser or moist sponge into each.

2
Give each child a piece of colored paper and access to at least two tubs of paint.

3
Let the children stamp and decorate the paper in any style they wish.

4
Once the prints are dry, cut them into pieces measuring approximately 3 x 4 inches (7.5 x 10 cm). The cuts can be irregular in shape and size.

5
Glue the printed pieces onto cards. Experiment with using blank pieces of paper or torn, corrugated cardboard as backgrounds and with adding twine or found objects to the arrangements.

6
Add the artist's name to the back of each card.

Variations

You can simplify this easy technique even more by using finger paints rather than stamps.

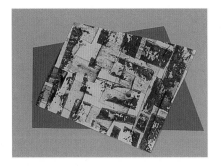

p.s.

Cards like these make wonderful fund-raisers for schools and other groups.

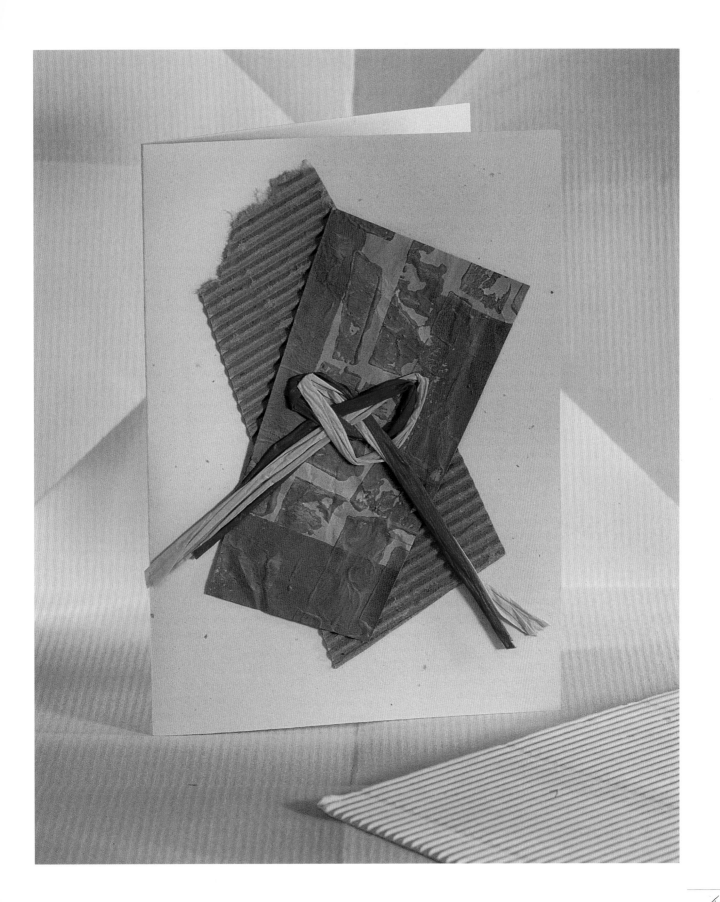

Designer: Lynn Krucke

This super-fancy showpiece card incorporates easy-to-use embossing powders, plus inks and lots of layering. The result: a background of luminous images framing a handmade "tile" in the center. You can find all the embossing supplies you need in the stamp section of any craft store.

What You Need

3 pieces of card stock in different but coordinating colors:

* 1 measuring 8^1/$_2$x 11 inches (21.3 x 27.5 cm), plus an extra scrap measuring 1 x 3^3/$_4$ inches (2.5 x 9.5 cm) (Navy was used in the design shown.)

* 1 measuring approximately 5 x 5 inches (12.5 x 12.5 cm) (Black was used in the design shown.)

* 1 measuring approximately 4 x 7 inches (10 x 17.5 cm) (Teal was used in the design shown.)

A scrap of mat board, trimmed to 2 x 3-^{1}/$_4$ inches (5 x 8.5 cm) (Dark blue was used in the design shown.)

Clear embossing ink

Pearlescent powdered mica in copper and blue-green (This paint in powdered form is used dry in this project. You can find it in art and craft supply stores.)

Spray fixative (Widely available in art and craft supply stores, this is the same product used to prevent a chalk or pastel drawing from smearing.)

Double-thick clear embossing powder

Stamp pad with copper pigment ink (Be sure to choose a pad with pigment ink rather than dry-based ink, which will dry before the embossing powder has a chance to cling to it.)

Copper embossing powder

Bone folder

Feather stamp

Paintbrush with soft bristles

Facial tissue

Ruler

Scissors or craft knife

Copper-colored metallic paint pen

Heat tool (available at craft stores; optional)

Small spoon (A plastic tester spoon from an ice cream parlor is perfect.)

"Happy Birthday" stamp

Double-stick tape

1

Fold the largest piece of card stock in half to create your card. Ink the feather stamp with clear embossing ink, and stamp it randomly on the front of card, stamping some images off the sides and varying the direction of the stamp as you go. (If you have trouble seeing where you've stamped, tilt the card at an angle as you work.)

2

Using the paintbrush, lightly dust copper-colored pearlescent powdered mica over the front of the card. The stamped images will emerge as the powder clings to the wet, stamped areas. Lightly buff the front of the card with facial tissue to remove any excess powder.

3

Repeat the process of stamping with clear embossing ink on the 5- x 5-inch (12.5 x 12.5 cm) piece of card stock and on the 4- x 7-inch (10 x 17.5 cm) piece of card stock. Use the blue-green pearlescent powdered mica to make the images emerge on the larger piece and the copper-colored pearlescent powdered mica on the smaller one.

4

Buff the smaller pieces with facial tissue as well, then spray all three pieces with fixative to prevent the powder from rubbing off.

5

Once the fixative is dry, cut the 5- x 5-inch (12.5 x 12.5 cm) piece of card stock into two pieces measuring 1^1/$_2$ x 4^1/$_4$ inches (3.8 x 11 cm) and 3^1/$_2$ x 4^3/$_4$ inches (8.8 x 12 cm). Cut the 4- x 7-inch (10 x 17.5 cm) piece of card stock into two pieces measuring 1^1/$_4$ x 3 inches (3.1 x 7.5 cm) and 2^1/$_2$ x 3^3/$_4$ inches (6.25 x 9.5 cm).

6

Use the copper-colored metallic paint pen to line edges of all the pieces created in step 5, and set them aside.

7

Ink the feather stamp with copper pigment ink, and set it aside.

8

Cover the small piece of mat board with clear embossing ink, then sprinkle the entire piece with double-thick clear embossing powder. Tap off the excess, and return it to the container.

9

Melt the powder by moving the heat tool in slow circles over the mat board. (If you don't have a heat tool, which gently blows very hot air, you can carefully hold the card over a stove burner, in front of a hot iron, or over a light bulb.) The first layer will appear bumpy when it's melted (somewhat like a linoleum floor). While the piece is still warm, sprinkle on another light layer of powder (this is where that ice cream spoon comes in handy!), and melt it. Continue this process, working on small areas at a time, until your "tile" is as thick as you want it (three to four layers is typically adequate).

10

Once you've finished layering the embossing powder and while the powder is still warm and soft, gently press the feather stamp into the tile. (This requires almost no pressure; the stamp will settle into the warm melted powder.) Allow the powder to cool, then remove the stamp. (The ink acts as a releasing agent, so the stamp should be easy to remove.) Spray the tile with fixative to set the pigment ink, and use the copper-colored metallic paint pen to color the sides of the mat board.

11

Ink the "Happy Birthday" stamp with copper pigment ink, and stamp the small scrap of card stock that matches your card. Sprinkle copper embossing powder over the image, tapping off any excess and returning it to the container. Emboss the image, again using a heat tool or one of the other methods described in step 9. Be sure to emboss the image completely. Any embossing powder that isn't melted will brush off.

12

Use double-stick tape to layer the pieces and attach them to the card, using the arrangement in the design shown as a guide.

Designer: Carol Pallesen

These mono-prints made with mat board are simple yet striking. The bold lines and spare design (inspired by gazing at patches of earth from an airplane, says the designer) suit scores of occasions.

What You Need

Card stock folded into a card or
a blank card

Scrap of mat board (easy to come by
at framing shops)

Watercolors

Scrap paper

Craft knife

Artist's brush

Fine-pointed pen with metallic ink

Commercial or handmade stamp
(optional)

1

Cut a square of mat board that measures 2 x 2 inches (5 x 5 cm).

2

If you want to avoid coating your fingers with paint when you stamp the card, fashion a little handle on the back of your square of mat. Simply peel two layers of paper from opposite corners of the square, and hold them where they meet in the middle.

3

Apply watercolor (in one solid color or several colors) to the front of the mat with the artist's brush. You want the paint to be somewhat watery, but not runny. Experiment with the consistency, and practice a few stamps on a piece of scrap paper. When you're happy with the results, stamp a couple of spots on the front of the card.

4

While the stamped area is still wet, you may want to add a bit of silver or gold paint for accent. Dab it onto the wet areas with the end of a brush; the added paint will create interesting patterns as it travels.

5

If you like, after the squares have dried completely, add a stamped image on top of them, such as the feather shown here.

6

Use the pen to write tiny alphabet letters—or any other message you choose—around the perimeter of the squares.

p.s.

When sending cards to fun-loving friends, make them piece the message together for themselves. Enclose a little something—maybe a photo or a written riddle—cut up into puzzle pieces and tossed inside the card like confetti. Could there be a more fittingly mysterious way to include the date, time, and place in a scavenger-hunt invitation?

Variation

Forget the mat board altogether, and measure and paint tiny boxes on your card, add details inside, and draw freehand lines around them.

"STAINED GLASS" BUTTERFLY

Designer: Lynn Krucke

With transparent, ultra-fine glitter, a clear window in the center of your card, and this clever decorative technique, you can simulate the luminous appeal of stained glass.

What You Need

3 pieces of card stock in different but coordinating colors:

* 1 measuring 5½ x 8½ inches (13.8 x 21.3 cm) (Duplex card stock that is sage-colored on the outside and cream-colored on the inside was used in the design shown.)

* 1 measuring 3¾ x 5 inches (9.5 x 12.5 cm) (Light olive stock was used in the design shown.)

* 1 measuring 3¼ x 4½ inches (8.1 x 11.3 cm) (You can also use handmade paper for this smallest piece; a light sage paper was used in the design shown.)

Acetate (A transparency from an office supply store is perfect.)

Ultra-fine glitter in colors to coordinate with your card stock (The designer of this project used dark brown and teal opaque glitter and light green, yellow, and lavender translucent glitter.)

Glue (For this project, it's important to use a glue that dries clear. You may also want one that goes on clear, so you can better monitor your application of glitter.)

Ink pad of black permanent ink

Bone Folder

Pencil

Ruler

Craft knife or scissors

Double-stick tape

Purchased or hand-carved stamp (Stamps with simple designs work best for this project.)

Spoon

Small paintbrush

1

Fold the largest piece of card stock in half to make the body of the card. On the center of the front panel, lightly mark an opening that is 3 inches (7.5 cm) wide and 3¼ inches (8.1 cm) long.

2

Open the card so that it lies flat, and use the craft knife to carefully cut out the rectangular opening.

3

Layer the two other pieces of card stock or paper, with the smaller piece in the center of the larger one. Use double-stick tape around the edges of the back of the smaller piece to secure it in place.

4

Treating the taped-together pieces as one, use the craft knife to cut an opening in the center measuring 2¾ inches (7 cm) wide and 3 inches (7.5 cm) long.

5

Ink the stamp with black permanent ink, and stamp your image onto the acetate. Let it dry thoroughly. (Patience pays off here! If the ink is not dry before you move on, it will smear when you apply the glue.)

6

Color your stamped image with glitter, making different sections different colors. First, apply glue to a section, staying inside the outline of the stamp. Then sprinkle or spoon the color of glitter you've chosen for that section over the glue, tapping off any excess glitter and returning it to the container. Use the paintbrush to brush away stray glitter. Allow each color to dry before moving to the next, working from darkest to lightest. When you're finished, set the piece aside to dry.

7

Once the image is dry, trim the acetate to approximately 3½ x 4 inches (8.8 x 10 cm). Cut a second piece of acetate the same size, and adhere it to the glittered side of the butterfly, using double-stick tape around the edges. (The front of the card will be the back of the butterfly. You'll see the glitter through the acetate, but it will be sealed inside.)

Using double-stick tape, mount the acetate piece on the front of the card, centering it in the opening. Tape the two-color frame you cut in step 4 to the front of the card, covering the taped acetate edges.

Designer: Margaret Desmond Dahm

The thrill of the hunt is at least half the fun of these endless-possibility cards. Scour hardware stores, fabric stores, toy stores, even grocery stores for pieces that will make interesting patterns when you print, from drain grills and coils of rope or chain to the tips of a hairbrush and the tires of a toy truck.

What You Need

1 piece of card stock, measuring 8 1/2 x 11 inches (21.3 x 27.5 cm)

Several scrap pieces of card stock or paper

Found object (Here, the designer shows variations using a plastic embroidery circle [facing page, right and bottom left], nylon fabric netting [facing page, bottom right], and lace pieces [facing page, upper left].)

Shallow plastic container for paint (The lid of a large yogurt container is perfect.)

Acrylic paints in various colors, including metallic colors

Paintbrush

Pencil colors (optional)

Masking tape

Ruler

Craft knife

1

Pour some paint into the plastic container, and thin it with water, if necessary, keeping in mind that the paint needs to be thick enough to move from the printing object to the paper without running.

2

Try some sample prints on one of the pieces of scrap paper. Tape the paper to your work surface, and experiment with two different printing methods. You can spread paint evenly over the surface of your printing object, press the painted surface onto the paper, then lift it off in a single, upward motion (to get a clear image). Or, you can lay the printing object on top of the paper and dab paint through it with the paintbrush. Play with printing on scrap paper until you get a feel for how your object prints and how much pressure and paint to use.

3

When you're ready to print your actual card, you can either print on the large sheet of card stock, then cut it to size once the print is dry, or cut

and fold your card first and just print on the front. Tape the card or sheet of card stock in place before you begin. (Here's a trick for treating your tape so that it's still sticky but won't tear your card stock when you remove it: Stick the tape to a clean piece of fabric and pull it back off before using it.)

4

If you want to overlay colors, let each print dry thoroughly before adding another.

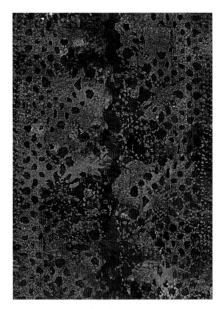

Lace print

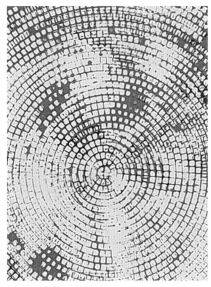

Plastic embroidery circle print

Variations

The designer painted the lace-print card (above, left) with a dark wash of blue and black acrylic paint and allowed it to dry before printing the lace in a lighter color on top.

The designer colored the cards (right) that feature prints of nylon netting with opaque pencil colors before printing on them. She also added card-stock frames after the prints were dry.

Nylon fabric netting prints

_G_USHY _G_REETINGS

A Sampling of Some of History's More Passionate and Complicated Pairs of Pen Pals

Peter Abelard & Heloise
1100s

Philosopher Peter Abelard fell in love with his 19-year-old student, Heloise, a French nun, and eventually they married. Heloise's uncle, Fulbert, didn't like the idea, so he ordered that Abelard be castrated. The couple was separated (Heloise was sent back to the convent, and Abelard traveled from monastery to monastery), but they continued to correspond, consoling each other with written words, for years.

Napoleon Bonaparte & Josephine Beauharnais
Late 1700s

Two days after the couple married in 1796, Napoleon went to war. Tormented by Josephine's consistent failure to respond to his letters (and by the knowledge that she was taking up with lovers), Napoleon grew bitter and eventually divorced her. Soon after, he struck up a correspondence with the Polish Countess Marie Walewska (considered his "great love"), and requested the hand of the 18-year-old Archduchess Marie-Louise of Austria.

Benjamin Franklin & Madame Brillon
Late 1700s

When in his seventies, Franklin was smitten with the flirtatious thirty-year-old, whom he met in Paris. They continued to correspond for years after Franklin returned to America.

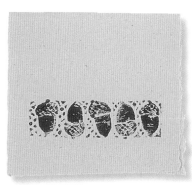

Copier

C ARDS

TORN IMAGES

Designer: Kate Harper

How satisfying to combine technology with timeless techniques. For these pretty handmade pieces, rough sketches make a pass through a photocopier before winding up on textured paper that is torn and added to a card.

What You Need

Card stock folded into a card or a blank card

Sheet of white paper

Variety of soft-colored recycled or textured paper

Black drawing tools (markers, pencils, crayons)

Scissors

Access to a photocopy machine

Glue

1

Use black drawing tools to sketch out several images on the sheet of white paper. Refer to patterns, pieces of clip art, or images from books or magazines as guides, if you like. (Remember that for this technique, rougher images are often more appealing, and the copying process adds a bit of polish to any design.)

2

Copy the images onto several different types and colors of paper.

3

Tear an image out of one of the sheets of paper.

4

Glue the image to the front of the card, and sign your name in black below it.

5

Repeat the process with the other images and paper colors.

Variation

Cut the image from the paper, then layer it on top of a piece of torn-paper backing.

Designer: Mardi Dover Letson

A high school science text is transformed into hip art once it's copied, dyed, and hand colored, then mounted on a card. Any similar illustration—think anatomical drawings, botanical prints, diagrams from cookbooks— can provide the raw material for a clever copy card.

1

Brush coffee onto the surface of the photocopy with the artist's brush, and allow it to dry. If the photocopy is not as dark as you'd like once it's dry, repeat the process as many times as necessary.

2

Trim the photocopy, if necessary, so that when it is mounted on the coordinating piece of paper, the paper will provide a slight (approximately 1/8-inch [3 mm]) frame.

3

Use colored pencils to tint the illustrations.

4

Brush the back of the photocopy with glue, and attach it to the frame, using the ruler to center it in place.

5

Use the same technique to attach the framed print to the front of your card.

What You Need

Card stock folded into a card or a blank card

A piece of paper or card stock for a frame (This paper should coordinate in color with your card and measure approximately 1/2 inch [1.3 cm] smaller in length and width than the front of your card.)

Black-and-white photocopied illustration

Strong coffee

Artist's brush

Craft knife or scissors

Colored pencils

Glue

Ruler

p.s.

Tea also makes a beautiful, more delicate, natural dye.

ished card a high-quality look and feel. Your original collage can be larger than the image that will appear on your cards (it's easier to work on that way; then you can reduce it on the copy machine). Just make sure the original collage is in correct proportion to the final copy size you want. For example, if you want the copied image to measure 4 x 6 inches (10 x 15 cm), your original collage should measure 8 x 12 inches (20 x 30 cm). You would then be able to reduce it 50 percent and end up with exactly the same image (without cutting off parts of the image or ending up with unnecessary white space).

1

Determine the size you want your finished, copied image to be, so you can make your original collage in a size that is proportional.

2

On the drawing paper, mark out the size you have to work with for your original collage, and create a central figure. In the project shown, the designer drew a female figure with a fine-point pencil, added a necklace with a soft-lead pencil, and used gouache paint (chosen for its quick-dry nature and brilliant color) to give her a billowy garment and matching lipstick and toenail polish. If you're not comfortable with your freehand drawing ability, use images from books or magazines as guides, or piece your figure together from clippings.

3

Use paints or pencils to shade the background around the central figure.

4

Glue on accents and a border. The cushions, hat, and aroma bottle in the project shown were clipped from fashion newsprint with chrome-coated stock. The border was made with strips cut from a catalogue of oriental carpets and from a scrap of paper from a cement bag.

5

Make as many color copies as you need, reducing the image to the finished size you've settled on.

6

Cut the card stock. Based on the approach you've chosen, you'll either cut out images to slip inside a premade window card or cut pieces to fold into cards.

7

On each copied image, add a bit of detail (glitter, sequins, ribbon, etc.). On the card shown, the designer cut tiny pieces of gold trim to create earrings on her figure.

8

Sign and date each card at the bottom.

Vellum Insert

Want to add a just-for-fun extra? Here's how to make light, airy fall-out sheets to insert inside your cards.

1

Determine the size you want your copied insert to be (the insert shown measures $3^1/_2$ x 6 inches [8.8 x 15 cm]) so that you can figure the size of your original, following the same procedure outlined at the beginning of the card instructions on the facing page.

2

On the second sheet of drawing paper, mark out the size you have to work with for your original collage. From the same decorative papers and other materials used for the card collage, cut a background piece and an image, such as the abstract tree shown here.

3

Glue the insert collage in place on the drawing paper.

4

Copy the insert collage onto vellum (reducing the size as necessary), and cut the insert images to size.

Designer: Mardi Dover Letson

Color copiers are no longer exotic. You can find them at nearly any corner copy shop, ready to help you transform real-life objects—from pretty pressed blooms to brilliant fall leaves—into vibrant cards.

What You Need

Pressed pansy bloom (or any other pressed flower or piece of foliage)

Tracing paper or white tissue paper

Decorative paper

Card made out of stiff, handmade paper that coordinates with the color of your bloom

Paper for inside greeting (Here, the designer used rice paper.)

Craft knife

Tape

Glue

Ruler

1

Make a color copy of the pansy bloom (you may choose to reduce or enlarge it), then cut the image out in a square that will fit nicely on the front of your card.

2

Wrap tracing paper or tissue paper around the square image, as if you were wrapping a package, and secure the paper in the back with a piece of single-sided tape.

3

From the decorative paper, cut a square frame that is approximately $1/16$ inch (1.5 mm) larger than the wrapped color copy. Glue the wrapped color copy to the decorative paper.

4

With the ruler, center the framed image on the front of the card, and glue it in place.

5

Cut a piece of paper to a size that is slightly smaller than your card, then fold it and insert it as a piece for your written message.

Variations

Play with color copies of plates from antique books, your own photographs, and other pieces of pressed foliage.

Fasten

  & FOLD

Designer: Nicole Tuggle

Apply a traditional bookbinding technique to the art of making cards, and the advantages are twofold. Outside, the hand-bound edge adds an interesting decorative feature. Inside, your card can include a series of pages (all bound into place). The design is perfect if you want your card to double as a mini-scrapbook with photos and mementos—or if you've simply got a lot to say.

What You Need

2 equal-size pieces of thick card stock (Choose a card stock with weight similar to that of a standard file folder. The stock in the design shown is cut in a 5 1/2-inch [13.8 cm] square.)

2 colors of decorative paper that contrast with each other (The design shown features neutral flecked paper and rusty brown paper.)

Plain text-weight paper for internal pages (optional) (This paper should be cut into squares slightly smaller than the squares of card stock.)

Thick sewing needle

Awl (optional)

Thread, string, or thin ribbon

Glue

Artist's brush

Ruler

Pencil

Scissors

1

Cover both pieces of card stock with one of the decorative papers. With each piece, coat one side with glue by brushing on a thin layer, then wrap the paper around it, as if you're wrapping a package, and glue the ends in place on the other side. Then, cut a square of paper to glue over the uncovered area on the other side. (The sides with the glued squares of paper will be your inside covers.)

2

On one edge of one of the paper-covered squares of card stock, measure in 1/2 inch (1.3 cm). Mark the measurement with a light pencil line, and fold the 1/2-inch (1.3 cm) flap of card stock over, first one direction, then the other, creating a flexible hinge. The hinge will serve as the left side of the front of the card.

3

Out of the second color of decorative paper, cut a 1-inch-wide (2.5 cm) strip that is the same length as the side of the card. (The paper color should contrast with the color of your stitching material. For example, if you're using white string, select a dark paper.) Fold the paper strip in half lengthwise, and glue it in place around the hinged flap you created in step 2.

4

Lightly mark dots at 1/2-inch (1.3 cm) intervals along the length of the flap.

5

Using an awl or a thick sewing needle, poke through each of the marks to form a hole. Place the cover of the card on top of the back of the card, and line up the two pieces evenly. With the pencil, mark through each hole to create a guide for a series of identical holes on the left edge of the back of the card, then poke through them. Repeat this process on any internal pages you want to insert in the card.

6

Hold both covers and any internal pages together to make sure that all the holes line up. Thread your stitching material through the needle, and begin a running stitch. Start at the back of the card, and sew through the bottom hole, coming through to the front (leaving an inch or so of string dangling for now at the back of the card). Bring your string or ribbon around the left edge of the card in an upward fashion, and come up through the back of the second hole and out the front. Continue the running stitch until the string comes out of the top hole. Then, reverse the direction. Bring the string or ribbon around the edge in a downward fashion, and come up through the back of the second hole and out the front. Continue the running stitch downward until you come around to the back of the bottom of the card. Tie the remaining thread in a knot and trim the excess. You can conceal the knot by poking it through the last hole with an awl or your needle.

7

To embellish the front of the card, cut a small frame out of card stock (the one shown measures 3 x 3 1/2 inches [7.5 x 8.8 cm] around and 1/2 inch [1.3 cm] thick). Cover the frame with the same paper you used on the hinge, gluing it in place, and glue the frame to the front of the card.

8

Insert something in the frame—a photo, a token, or a word or phrase.

p.s.

If you're an incurable romantic, don't hold back when it comes to cards. Dab a drop of your signature scent on a cotton ball and toss it in the box where you keep your cards and stationery. Everything you send will smell faintly of you.

Designer: Annie Cicale

Keep your eye on the money—and watch it move! This classic magic-trick card uses a clever set of paper hinges to create a crafty optical illusion. A bit of strategic positioning and gluing, and abracadabra: The bill or check you slip inside appears to flip its position, depending on which way you open the card.

What You Need

2 pieces of card stock, cut to 3 x 6¹/2 inches (7.5 x 16.3 cm)

4 strips of decorative paper, cut to 1 x 5 inches (2.5 x 12.5 cm)

Glue

Artist's brush

Scrap paper

1

Lay the strips of decorative paper over and under the pieces of card stock, using figure 1 as a guide. Fold the ends of the four strips over to the outside, as indicated.

2

Glue the eight ends of the four strips in place on the outside of the card, following the illustration in figure 2. The best way to do this is to leave everything in place, and use a small scrap of paper as a glue guard to protect the card area underneath each strip as you apply glue. Brush glue on the end of one strip at a time, then remove the guard and press the end in place on the outside of the card. Continue until you have glued all of the ends in place.

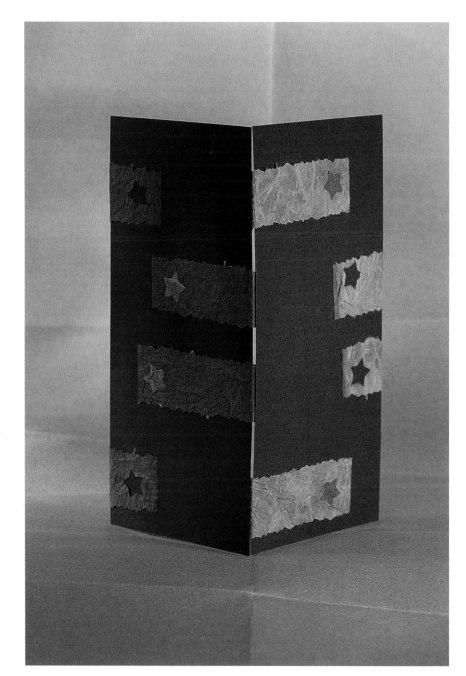

Figure 1. Inside view

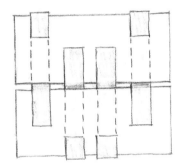

Figure 2. Outside view

Figure 3

3

Slip a bill or a check you want to send as a gift under one set of strips inside the card (see figure 3), and let the magic begin.

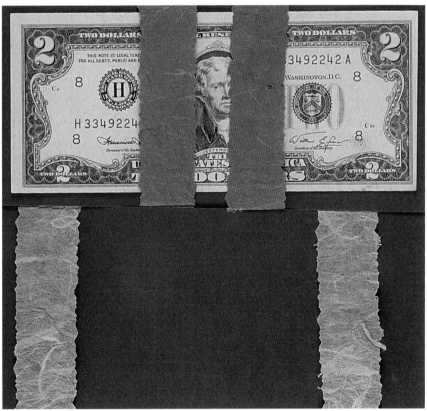

Designer: Allison Stilwell

Tug on the enticing little streamers poking out of this birthday box, and a full-blown celebration unfolds. Hard to match if you're sending wishes for festivity and fun.

What You Need

Matchbox

Acrylic paint

Permanent black marker, fine tip

Message strip measuring approximately 10 inches (25 cm) long (Your words can be computer generated, handwritten, or clipped from a magazine and glued together.)

Colored paper

Paintbrush

Scissors

Glue

1

Paint the two parts of the matchbox in bright colors and playful designs. For the project shown, the designer used gold paint with purple polka dots for the inside of the box and turquoise for the outside. She painted the outside cover with blue stripes on the edges and purple on the top, then added a birthday cake.

2

Once the paint is dry, use the black marker to add detail, outlining design elements (such as the cake) and adding a greeting to the top of the box.

3

Create your message strip (here, the designer printed the words to the song, *Happy Birthday*). If you're printing your message from a computer, use the "landscape" mode, which allows you to print down the length of a page rather than across it. Otherwise, use glue to attach segments of your message together into a complete strip that is approximately 10 inches (25 cm) long, and cut the strip so that it is about $1/2$ inch (1.3 cm) wide.

4

Fold the message, accordion style, so it will fit inside the box. If you like, glue an image to the bottom of the inside of the box (such as the clip-art hand, shown here), then glue the end of the message strip to the image or to the bottom of the box.

5

Cut small pieces of colored paper into swirls for ribbon, and add them to the outside end of the message strip. Allow them to stick, invitingly, out of the end of the closed box.

Designer: Annie Cicale

If you had a pretty little pouch on the front of your card, imagine the miniature mementos you could tuck inside: a pressed flower, a special stamp, a lock of hair. This simple pocket opens like a lotus blossom to receive whatever tiny treasure you choose, then folds up flat to hold it safely inside.

What You Need

Card stock folded into a card or a blank card

Translucent or decorative paper

Confetti or glitter (optional)

Craft knife

Pencil

Ruler

Glue

1

Use the template in figure 1 to cut a pouch out of the translucent or decorative paper (see Transferring Patterns, page 19). You can adjust the size of the pouch (so it suits the size of your card and easily accommodates whatever you plan to stick inside) by reducing or enlarging the template on a photocopy machine. You can also square the flaps and/or edge them in some way.

2

Center the square bottom of the pouch on the front of your card, and glue it in place. If you're using translucent paper, consider gluing glitter or confetti under the box for added effect.

3

Insert your memento of choice (tacking it with glue if you don't intend for the recipient to remove it).

4

To close the pouch, fold each flap down, working clockwise, then lift the corner of the first flap and tuck the corner of the last flap underneath. For added surprise, toss confetti into the pouch before sealing it up.

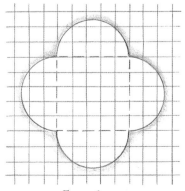

Figure 1

Variations

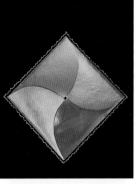

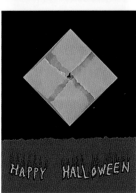

Designer: Terry Taylor

Honestly, now. If you received a package like this, would you ever, ever part with it? Not on your life. The opulent work of art would remain on permanent display. Create a rich keepsake just like it, and it will be treasured for all time.

What You Need

Screen wire measuring 4½ x 10 inches (11.3 x 25 cm)

Thin beading wire (about 16 inches [40 cm])

Vellum paper measuring 4½ x 10 inches (11.3 x 25 cm)

Single-face corrugated paper measuring 5 x 11 inches (12.5 x 27.5 cm)

Decorative ribbon (at least 12 inches [30 cm])

Assorted beads (seed beads, pony beads, glass and metal beads)

Ruler

Pencil

Scissors

Craft knife

Hole punch or grommet punch and grommets (Grommets are eyelets of firm material that protect a punched opening. Both grommets and grommet punches are available at most fabric and sewing supply stores.)

Awl or large needle

Beading needle (optional)

1

Gently fold the screen wire in half to form a card that measures 4½ x 5 inches (11.3 x 12.5 cm).

2

Crease the vellum in half to fit inside the screen, then place it inside, working it until it fits snugly in the fold.

3

Open the screen-and-vellum card, and on the inside fold, make three marks that are equal distances apart. Pierce the marks with the awl or needle.

4

You'll use a variation of a three-hole stitch (described in detail on page 98) to bind the spine of your card with beaded wire. You can use a beading needle if you like, but you'll probably find that the wire is stiff enough to thread through the beads and holes without it. Begin by threading the wire from the inside of the card through the center hole, leaving a tail of about 2 inches (5 cm).

5

Thread beads onto the wire until you reach the bottom hole, then thread the wire through the hole and bring it up to the tail. Twist the long piece of wire to the tail, creating tension on the row of beads you've just strung until they form an edge you're happy with.

6

Work the long piece of wire up to the top hole, thread it through to the outside, and string another set of beads until you reach the center hole.

7

Thread the end of the wire through the center hole, twist the end onto the tail, again, creating tension, then snip it closely with scissors.

8

Place the wire card on the corrugated paper, and fold the paper to enclose the card. There should be a slight overlap.

9

Use a pencil to lightly mark the position for the holes or grommets (they should be on either side of the overlap, roughly 1 inch [2.5 cm] apart). Use a hole punch or a grommet punch to make the holes.

10

Thread the decorative ribbon through the holes, from the back to the front, and tie it in a bow, or knot the ribbon loosely.

11

Write your message on the vellum and slip the card into the case.

This wire card is inserted in the presentation case.

Designer: Lynn Krucke

A few folded tabs and some strategically placed slits, and you've got a card that swings. This classic pop-up design never fails to delight—and it's perfect for cards that celebrate a holiday that thrives on surprise!

What You Need

Black card stock, 1 piece measuring 6¼ x 5½ inches (16 x 13.8 cm) and another measuring 1¾ inches (4.5 cm) square

1 piece of orange glossy card stock

Scrap paper measuring 3 x 3¾ inches (7.5 x 9.5 cm)

Acetate or lightweight cardboard (cereal boxes work fine) for making a template (optional)

White pigment ink

White embossing powder

White webbing spray

Pencil

Ruler

Craft knife

Bone folder

Halloween stamps (In the project shown, the designer used a skeleton stamp, a spiderweb stamp, and a "Trick or Treat" stamp.)

Heat tool (available at craft stores; optional)

Corner edgers

Double-stick tape

White paint pen

1

Transfer the card pattern, shown in figure 1, directly onto the larger piece of black card stock or to template material, which you can use as a guide for marking the pattern on the card stock (see Transferring Patterns, page 19). The pattern should be centered on the card stock, with the tab ends touching the edges of the longer sides.

2

Use the bone folder to score the fold lines and the craft knife to cut around the pattern's center rectangle, freeing the area that will swing.

3

Make one mountain and one valley fold, following the symbols on the pattern. As you make the folds, the center rectangle of the card will flip. When you open the folds back up, the center rectangle lies flat.

4

Ink one of the stamps (such as the skeleton in the project shown) with white pigment ink. With the card open and flat, stamp the skeleton on the center rectangle on the back of the card. (Note that when the card is folded, this back piece flips to the front. You may want your stamp to be slightly off center so that it appears in the appropriate position when it flips. Experiment with placement before stamping the image.)

5

Sprinkle white embossing powder onto the stamped image, tapping off the excess and returning it to its container. Use the heat tool to emboss the image, moving the tool in slow circles over the image to bring it out. (If you don't have a heat tool, which gently blows very hot air, you can carefully hold the card over a stove burner, in front of a hot iron, or over a light bulb.)

6

Once the back image is embossed, turn the card back over to the front. Use the piece of scrap paper as a mask to protect the center rectangle, ink another stamp (such as the spiderweb stamp in the project shown) with white pigment ink, and stamp randomly around the border of the card. Vary the angle of the stamp as you go, and stamp some images off the sides for more interest.

7

Spray the orange glossy card stock with white webbing spray until you like the look. Set it aside to dry.

8

Ink a third stamp (such as the "Trick or Treat" stamp in the project shown) with white pigment ink, and stamp the smaller piece of black card stock.

fold; the two others should each be ¹/₄ inch (1 cm) in from each edge (see figure 3). Thread the needle with the waxed linen thread, insert it from the outside of the envelope, coming up through the center hole. Go out through one of the side holes, along the outside spine of the envelope, back up through the other side hole, and down through the center hole one final time (see figure 4). Knot the ends of the thread, and leave a tail.

5

Sew a bead or button to the outside of the top flap, then wrap the tail of waxed linen thread around it to seal the envelope shut.

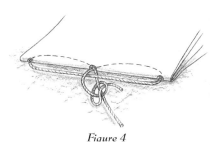

Figure 4

FOLDED SQUARE ENVELOPE & CARD

1

Fold the text-weight paper in half, creating a folded piece that measures 4 x 6 inches (10 x 15 cm). Crease the fold with the bone folder.

2

Diagonally position the folded text-weight paper inside the decorative paper (see figure 5), and fold the corners of the decorative paper inward, creasing the folds with the bone folder.

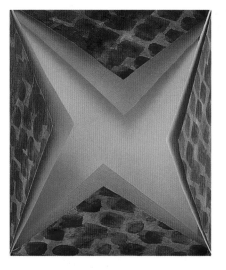

3

Use the same three-hole stitch described in step 4, facing page, to attach the text-weight paper to the decorative-paper envelope, or glue the text-weight paper in place. (See figure 6.)

4

Use a sticker seal to hold your envelope shut.

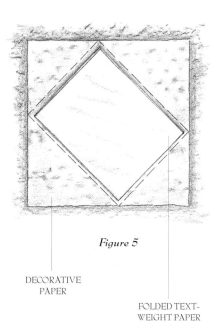

Figure 5

DECORATIVE PAPER

FOLDED TEXT-WEIGHT PAPER

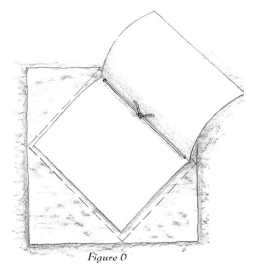

Figure 6

Variations:

* Instead of using a button or bead to tie your Tri-fold Envelope & Card shut, create a slot for tucking the top flap into the bottom one. On the bottom flap, measure in from the end 2¹/₂ inches (6.25 cm), make two pencil dots approximately 4¹/₂ inches (11.3 cm) apart, and, with the ruler as a guide, use the craft knife to cut a straight slit between the two dots (see figure 7).

* Use two layers of decorative paper to add depth to your design and weight to more fragile, handmade papers.

* Begin the three-hole stitch from the inside of the card, so the decorative knot rests against the text-weight paper inside.

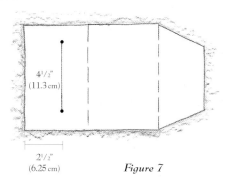

4¹/₂" (11.3 cm)

2¹/₂" (6.25 cm)

Figure 7

Designer: Tracy Page Stilwell

Want to feed creativity, encourage action, or let someone know you believe in her in a big way? Then your message might as well be delivered with a burst of enthusiasm. Bright batik prints and a handful of folds are just the thing.

What You Need

Sheet of watercolor paper

Rubber cement

Watercolor paints

1 piece of paper, 8 x 16 inches (20 x 40 cm)

Computer-generated copy cut into separate words (You can also use words clipped from magazines or copied from books or use rubber-stamped words.)

Scraps of tissue paper

Red paper cut in the shape of a small heart

Stencils in the shapes of triangles, moons, spirals, or anything else you like (You can purchase these or create your own.)

Artist's brush

Pencil

Ruler

Small sponge

Scissors or craft knife

Bone folder

Glue

Making Batik Paper

1

Apply rubber cement to the watercolor paper in drips, drizzles, and blobs, and let it dry.

2

With an artist's brush, brush watercolor paint in random patterns over the cement-decorated paper, and let it dry.

3

You can repeat steps 1 and 2 as many times as you like, using new colors of paint in new patterns each time. For the project shown, the designer applied three rounds of rubber cement and paint.

4

When the paint and rubber cement are completely dry, peel and/or rub the cement off the paper, and your pattern will emerge.

Creating the Card

1

Cut two 4-inch (10 cm) squares from your batik paper.

2

Using a pencil and a ruler, make light guide marks on the 8- x 16-inch (20 x 40 cm) piece of paper for eight 4-inch (10 cm) squares.

3

Following the illustration in figure 1, use a craft knife or scissors to cut along the cut lines, then use your ruler and bone folder to make crisp folds along the remaining lines.

4

Glue your batik squares in position on the 8- x 16-inch (20 x 40 cm) piece of paper, using figure 1 as a guide.

5

Glue your words in order in all the squares that aren't backed by batik squares.

6

Use the sponge and stencils to apply watercolor paint in random patterns. (As an alternative, acrylic paint works just as well.)

7

Add a heart on top of a scrap of tissue to the final square.

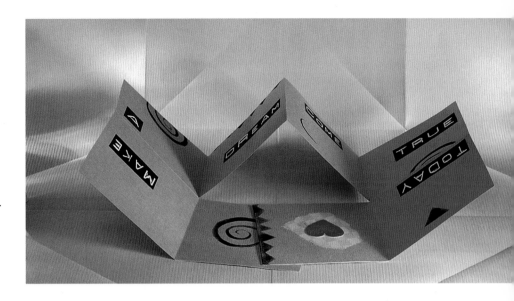

The card folds so that the two batik squares form the front and back covers. The recipient can flip through the squares (like the pages of a book) to read the message, then unfold the entire piece for a happy explosion of words and imagery.

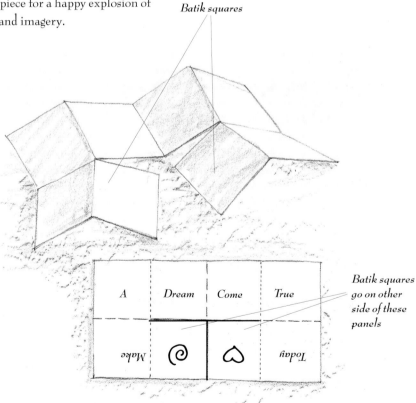

Batik squares

Batik squares go on other side of these panels

A	Dream	Come	True
Make	@	♡	Today

Figure 1

Designer: Nicole Tuggle

Whatever's inside has got to be worth reading—why else would it be sealed so carefully? There's nothing better than a clever closure to pique your pen pal's curiosity about what you've got to say.

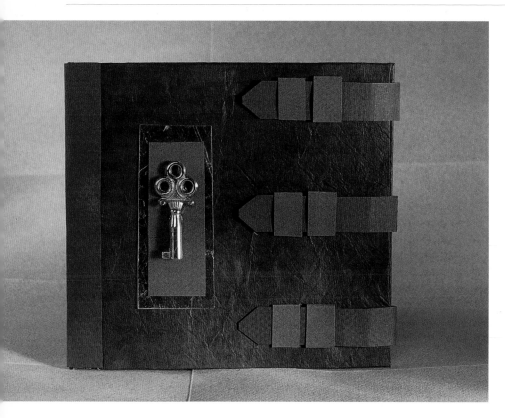

What You Need

Thick, flexible decorative paper in two colors that coordinate with each other and with the color of your card

Card stock folded into a card or a blank card

Decorative token or found object (optional)

Glue

Scissors

Ruler

1

Cut three strips of paper that measure 5½ inches (13.8 cm) long and ½ inch (1.3 cm) wide. Snip the ends at an angle to form half-diamond shapes. (This narrowed shape helps the strips move through the buckles later.)

2

Fold each strip in half, making sure the folds are in identical spots on each strip.

3

Glue the non-angled ends of the three strips along the back side of the card, perpendicular to the opening. Glue the first one in the center and the other two 1 inch (2.5 cm) away from the center strip on either side.

4

Coax the strips around the card and press them flat against the surface of the front. (Don't worry if they pop back up instead of resting flat. The buckles you make in the next step will hold them in place.)

5

To make the buckles, cut six strips of paper ½ inch (1.3 cm) wide and approximately 1½ inches (3.8 cm) long. Fold them into loops that allow the strips to pass freely but snugly through.

6

Glue down a first set of three loops 1 inch (2.5 cm) from the open edge of the card. Glue the next set of three loops just beyond the first set (toward the middle of the card), so you end up with three rows consisting of two loops each.

7

Embellish the front of the card, if you like. Here, the designer used a rectangle of mica, a paper scrap, and a simple found object.

THIS WAY, THAT WAY

Designer: Carol Palleson

with special thanks to Hedi Kyle, whose book design inspired the card

This way, that way, any way you look at it, this concertina-fold card with flip-flop flaps
is a piece of correspondence that bursts with celebration.

What You Need

4 pieces of card stock (you can choose
3 different colors, if you wish):

* 1 measuring 4 x 7¹/₂ inches
(10 x 18.8 cm) (for concertina)

* 2 measuring 4 x 8¹/₂ inches
(10 x 21.3 cm) (for covers)

* 1 measuring 3³/₄ x 12 inches
(9.5 x 30 cm) (for flap strips)

Bone folder

Double-stick tape

Craft knife

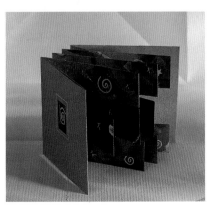

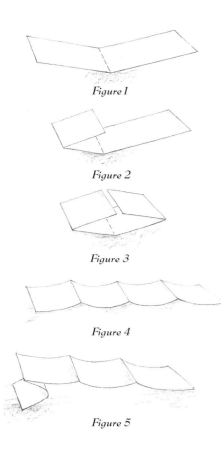

Figure 1

Figure 2

Figure 3

Figure 4

Figure 5

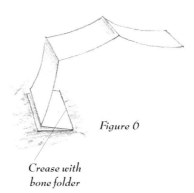

Figure 6

Crease with bone folder

Press lightly to begin each fold (see figure 5), then crease the fold underneath with the bone folder. (See figure 6.) Keep the fold edges aligned with the edge of the paper as you work. (See figure 7.) (It helps to hold your head directly over your work, looking straight down on the card.)

Finally, use a valley fold to fold the end in.

2

Fold each of the two pieces to be used for your covers in half. Apply double-stick tape to both sides of both ends of the concertina-fold piece (close to the folds), and attach the front and back cover pieces. (See figure 8). Burnish the places where the covers adhere to the folds with the bone folder.

1

Starting with the 4- x 7^{1}/$_{2}$-inch (10 x 18.8 cm) piece of card stock, use a technique those in card-crafting circles call a "wave-to-shore" concertina fold to create the center of your card. It's illustrated in figures 1-3. (This is one of the most accurate ways to get perfectly aligned panels.)

First, fold the paper in half precisely, then unfold it. Next, fold both ends into the middle fold line, and unfold them. (See figures 1-3.)

Turn the paper over. Think of the three rising mountain folds you created (see figure 4) as three waves you want to bring to shore by folding them in.

3

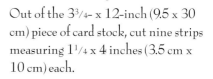

Out of the 3^{3}/$_{4}$- x 12-inch (9.5 x 30 cm) piece of card stock, cut nine strips measuring 1^{1}/$_{4}$ x 4 inches (3.5 cm x 10 cm) each.

4

Attach the strips to the concertina-fold piece, using the x marks in figure 9 as a guide. Use double-stick tape to attach each strip, then burnish it in place.

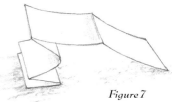

Figure 7

Variation

For added flair, decorate the strips before taping them in place. In the project shown, the designer painted the strips first, rubber-stamped them with silver ink, and made tiny cutouts with a star hole punch. She also cut a window in the front cover of the card before attaching it, and backed it with a decorative piece of paper.

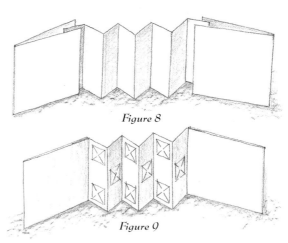

Figure 8

Figure 9

POP ART HEARTS

Designer: Annie Cicale

Once you get the hang of this card that bursts with greetings, you can make variations featuring a splendid array of shapes, from Christmas trees to soccer balls.

What You Need

1 piece of card stock measuring 6¼ x 18 inches (16 x 45 cm)

2 pieces of colored card stock, each measuring 4½ x 6¾ inches (11.3 x 16.9 cm)

Assortment of decorative paper

Ribbon

Bone folder

Pencil

Craft knife

Scissors

Glue

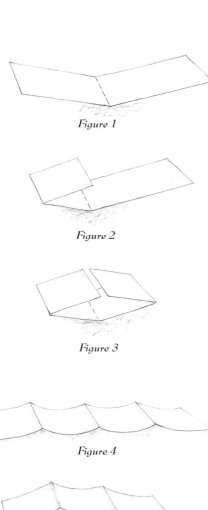

Figure 1

Figure 2

Figure 3

Figure 4

Figure 5

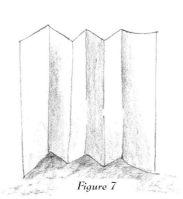

Figure 6

Figure 7

Figure 8

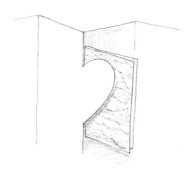

Figure 9

Figure 10

Figure 11

1

Fold the card stock in a variation of the waves-to-shore concertina fold described in the This Way, That Way project on page 103.

First, fold the paper in half precisely, then unfold it. Next, fold both ends into the middle fold line, and unfold them. (See figures 1-3.)

Turn the paper over, and you'll have three mountain folds. (See figure 4.) Tuck the first panel underneath the folds. (This piece will become the front of your card.) (See figure 5.)

Think of the other two peaks as waves you want to bring to shore by folding them in. Press lightly to begin each fold, then crease the fold underneath with the bone folder. Keep the fold edges aligned with the edge of the paper as you work. (See figure 6.)

When you finish, as you look at the inside of your card, you will see two mountain folds bordered by front and back panels. (See figure 7.)

2

On each of the two mountain folds in what will be the inside of your card, draw three heart halves, using the fold as the center line. Alternate the heart halves from one side of the fold to the other, and vary their size (see figure 8). Cut out the heart halves with the craft knife, and pop each half away from the panel.

3

Fold a small scrap of decorative paper in half, and place it under one of the heart halves you cut out in step 2, with the fold of the scrap against the fold of the card. Trace around the shape of the heart, and cut a whole

heart of the decorative paper (see figures 9 and 10). Glue the decorative-paper heart over the pop-out heart, as shown in the project photo, making sure the edges adhere well. You may want to glue decorative paper hearts on both sides of the pop-out shape, using a different paper on each side.

4

Glue one of the pieces of colored card stock onto the card's front cover. Before gluing the other piece on the back, glue the ribbon across the middle of the back panel, so the ends can wrap around the front and tie.

Variation

....

If you want hearts that pop out of both panels inside your card, draw whole hearts, with the sides offset about 1/8 inch (3 mm). (See figure 11.) The strip

you create by offsetting the sides keeps the heart in place (so be careful to leave it intact when you cut out the heart). Since these hearts are often asymmetrical, you'll want to trace each side individually on the decorative paper you use to cover it, then adjust at the fold to smooth out the curves.

p.s.

Here's a graceful way to coax a response from your card's recipient: Cut a small swatch from a pretty piece of tissue paper, fold it in half, place a favorite, unused stamp inside, and insert it—with anticipation— in your card.

Designer: Annie Cicale

Tasteful wrapping dresses up everything from packages to candy—why not cards? Whether you're inserting a printed invitation or folding up multiple pieces to slip inside (maybe an RSVP card and a map to the wedding reception) these wonderful wrappers with interlocking closures make the message all the more special.

What You Need

Material for template (Cardboard and acetate both work well.)

Card stock or heavy decorative paper that coordinates with your enclosure

Pencil

Ruler

Craft knife or scissors

1

Determine the size (including dimensions and thickness) of what you want to put inside your wrapper, then adapt one of the patterns in figure 1 to make your own template out of cardboard or acetate. To gauge the length of the rectangular area of the template (which must wrap around whatever you plan to put inside), use a narrow strip of paper as you would a measuring tape, wrapping it around the folded card (or whatever else you will put inside the wrapper). Mark the point where the strip overlaps (see figure 2). Unwrap it, and use that distance to plot the length of the rectangle. The rectangle should also measure slightly more in height than the card, so it will neatly cover the card's top and bottom edges.

2

From each outer edge of the rectangle, measure in one-fourth the width to determine where you will make valley folds.

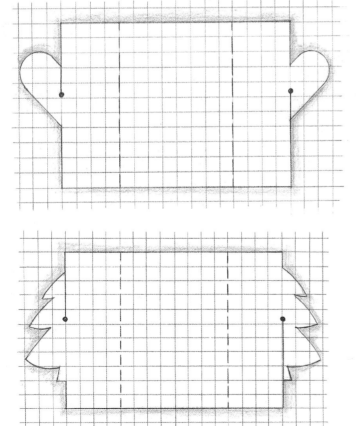

Figure 1

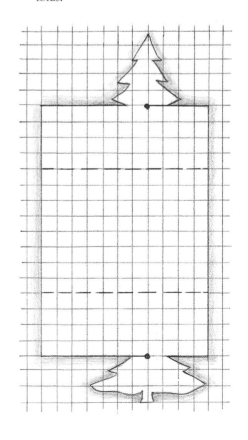

3

On either side of the rectangle on the template, add a symmetrical shape. When locked together, the two shapes will form your closure (which might be a Christmas tree or a heart, for example). Use the patterns in figure 1 as a guide for creating the symmetrical shapes.

4

Use your template to transfer the pattern to the wrong side (if any) of the card stock or decorative paper (tracing onto what will be the inside of the wrapper), and cut out the design with the craft knife.

5

Where the symmetrical shape meets the edge of the rectangle on one side, slit a line from the top of the shape to the middle. On the other side, slit a line from the bottom of the shape to the middle. Use the cut lines on the patterns as a guide.

6

To assemble the wrapper, fold one of the flaps in. Bring the two parts of the closure symbol together and slide one slit into the other. Then, press down on the wrapper and lightly crease the second fold, making sure that the top and bottom of the wrapper align. Slip your enclosure into the wrapper after the slits have been slipped together.

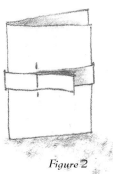

Figure 2

Variation

Make the wrapper's closure stand out by covering it with another color of decorative paper, like the designer did with the green Christmas tree and the red heart.

Gift
CARDS

Designer: Tracy Page Stilwell

Give a gift of gumption. This triple-fold pack has an inside pocket brimming with bits of inspiration ripe
for the recipient's picking and choosing.

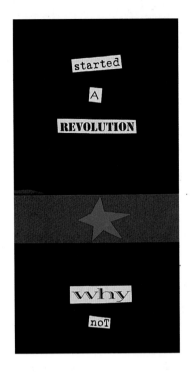

What You Need

1 piece of black card stock measuring
5 x 15 inches (12.5 x 37.5 cm)

1 piece of black card stock measuring
3 x 5¹/₂ inches (7.5 x 13.8 cm)

1 piece of green card stock measuring
2¹/₂ x 5 inches (6.25 x 12.5 cm)

Scraps of red, green, and black card stock
(or other colors of your choosing)

Photocopies or computer-generated ver-
sions of a photograph and words like the
ones shown in this design—or of those
that communicate your own "revolution-
ary" message

Pencil

Ruler

Bone folder

Glue

Scissors and/or craft knife

1

On your largest piece of card stock,
mark two 5-inch (12.5 cm) intervals,
and make folds with the bone folder so
the bottom panel folds up and the top
panel folds down.

2

Fold the strip of green card stock in half,
and glue it to the bottom edge of the
bottom panel of the triple-fold piece,
making a 1¹/₄-inch (3.5 cm) border on
both sides of the panel.

3

Trim the photo and words for your
main message, and glue them to the
card, paying attention to the direction
of the card's folds.

4

Use the pattern in figure 1 to cut the
card's pocket out of your 3- x 5¹/₂-inch
(7.5 x 13.8 cm) piece of black card stock.
With a ruler and pencil, mark the flaps,
then use your bone folder to crease
them so they fold in the same direction.

5

Glue the bottom flap of the pocket to
the inside of the card's middle panel;
wrap the side flaps around the sides, and
glue them to the outside of the panel.

6

Cut and glue a heart on the front of
the pocket, a star on the border of the
outside of the bottom panel, and strips
of green and red paper in random spots
anywhere you like them.

7

Glue your inspirational words on
1-inch (2.5 cm) strips of various colors
of card stock, let them dry, and pack
them in the pocket.

Figure 1

Today, handmade cards (along with their commercial counterparts) commonly travel by truck, train, boat, and plane to reach their destinations. But throughout history, messages have journeyed to mailboxes in many ways.

■ Camels have been used for mail delivery in desert regions around the world. In 1857, the United States experimented with camels imported from the Middle East as a way to deliver mail to military posts and settlements in the desert southwest. But not all deserts are the same, it seems. After a difficult trial period, the camels were dismissed from service.

■ Both carrier pigeons and hot-air balloons were used by besieged Parisians during the Franco-Prussian war in 1870.

■ Despite their reputation as a threat to safe mail delivery, dogs have also been letter carriers' best friends. Dogsleds have long been used to transport mail across arctic regions. Many individual dogs have helped as well. "Dorsey" hauled mail in saddle bags in Bismarck, North Dakota, at the turn of the century, and "Shep," a hound-dog mutt, took mail to the upper floors of buildings along his carrier's route in Chanute, Kansas, from 1911 to 1913.

■ In remote areas of the French Alps, mail has been delivered on skis, and snowshoes and snowmobiles are used by mail carriers in northern regions of various countries.

■ Stilts have been used to traverse marshy areas when delivering mail in Landes, France.

■ The Jackass Mail Line existed in 1857 to carry mail between San Francisco and Los Angeles, California. Today, mules carry mail down a steep, eight-mile trail to the Native American inhabitants of Supai, Arizona, below the south rim of the Grand Canyon.

■ Everywhere from France to Florida, floating balls have been used to send cards and messages downriver.

■ Pneumatic tubes and metal canisters were used in the late 1800s in Germany, France, and the United States for fast, underground mail service in large cities.

Mail being delivered by dogsled in Alaska

■ In the 1940s, the U.S. Navy placed a note in a bottle and set the experiment adrift in the Pacific Ocean. The bottle traveled 1,250 miles (2,010 km) in 53 days, finally landing in the New Hebrides Islands (today the Republic of Vanuatu).

SEEDY HEART

Designer: Susan L'Hommedieu

Not seedy as in disreputable—seedy as in agricultural! The unassuming little heart on the front of this card is a flower-patch-to-be. All it needs is soil, water, and sunlight.

What You Need

Card stock folded into a card or a blank card

2 pieces of card stock in coordinating colors

Flower seeds

Glue (Choose PVA glue, which dissolves in water.)

Card

Ruler

Pen

1

From each of the pieces of coordinating card stock, cut a rectangle (one smaller than the other). When layered, the two should fit easily on the front of the card. The rectangles in the project shown measure $2^{1}/_{2}$ x 4 inches (6.25 x 10 cm) and $1^{3}/_{4}$ x $2^{1}/_{4}$inches (4.5 x 5.6 cm).

2

On the smaller rectangle, draw the outline of a heart with glue, then fill it in with glue.

3

Sprinkle the flower seeds onto the wet glue, and pat them down gently to secure them in place.

4

Glue the seed-covered rectangle to the larger rectangle. Then center both on the front of the card and glue everything in place.

5

On the back of the card write *Plant This Card!*, and add the name of the seeds and their growing information (such as sun/shade preference, etc.). The card can be torn into small pieces and planted. After it's watered, the paper will soften and the glue will dissolve.

■ Some of the world's earliest greetings were written on tribal message sticks, on feathers, and on tablets of bronze, clay, or wax. In ancient Persia, clay "cards" were even carried in clay "envelopes."

■ New Year's goes down in history as the first card-giving holiday. In honor of the annual celebration, Egyptians hand-delivered gifts along with good wishes lettered on papyrus. The Romans engraved their New Year's greetings on copper pennies; German woodcuts commemorating the New Year date to the middle 15th century.

■ As early as the 1600s Native Americans in North America burned messages onto buckskin and bark and carved images on small blocks of wood to invite neighbors to feasts and celebrations.

■ Other early greetings weren't written at all. Smoke signals have been used all over the world not only in warfare, but also for calling together community members for social events. Drums were beaten in specific patterns to

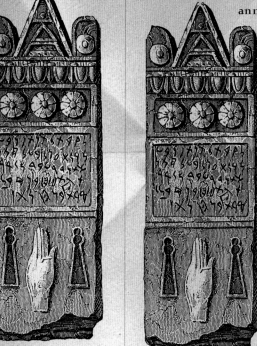

announce births and deaths in traditional Ugandan culture. And ringing church bells were the only wedding invitation needed in small European villages.

■ In early Sinhalese culture, news of a community member's death was sent with a lock of the deceased's hair wound around a twig and wrapped in leaves or cloth.

■ Handwritten invitations were de rigueur in royal courts throughout Europe during Renaissance times. Messages were elaborately lettered on large scrolls (often in colored ink embellished with large letter stamps) and delivered by pages, who would unroll the messages before the recipients and read them aloud. Strict rules of etiquette applied. A message was to be written on the largest sheet of paper available, with the recipient's title taking up at least five lines at the top of the page. The rest of the page was to be left blank—except for the very bottom, where it was appropriate for one's humble message to appear.

Designer: Barbara Bussolari

If you're pinning your hopes on a positive response, this striking gift and card in one is a sure bet. The removable pin is both a stunning part of the card itself and a classy keepsake.

What You Need

Card stock folded into a card or a blank card (For the project shown, the designer used a purchased white card with black deckle.)

Small section of mat board (This thin, sturdy board, available at art and craft stores, is most commonly used for framing and matting photographs.)

Assortment of thin, decorative paper

Acrylic medium (a clear varnish available at art and craft stores)

Buttons and/or beads of your choice

Natural material (Dried lichen—that fascinating fungus that grows on trees—is featured here, but you could use anything from seeds to pods.)

Pin back (available in craft and jewelry supply stores)

Pencil

Ruler

Black marker

Craft glue and a superglue

Craft knife

Artist's brush

Scissors

1

Use your craft knife to cut the mat board to the size you want the pin to be (the one shown measures 2 x 2¼ inches [5 x 5.6 cm]).

2

With the black marker, color the outside edges of the mat board, giving them a more finished look.

3

Cut or tear two pieces of decorative paper to fit the mat board, and glue them in place, covering both sides of the board. For added dimension, you can cut several more pieces of mat board, mark their sides, cover the tops with paper, and layer them on top of the larger piece, as shown here.

4

Cover all of the exposed sides of paper with several coats of acrylic medium, applying it with an artist's brush. The acrylic helps to hold the paper down, and it acts as a varnish, providing your pin with a finished look.

5

Add your beads, buttons, and natural materials, using superglue. Be sure whatever natural materials you're using are thoroughly dry before you attach them (spreading them out on newspaper for several days helps).

6

Glue the pin back to your pin design.

7

Cut or tear pieces of decorative paper that coordinate with those used on the pin, and play with their arrangement on the front of the card. Since the pin will be a part of the finished design, hold it up and consider its placement,

as well, as you play with the papers. Once you've settled on the design, glue the papers in place.

8

Lightly mark where the pin will attach to the card with a pencil, then use your craft knife to cut two ¼-inch (.6 cm) slots running up and down about 1 inch (2.5 cm) apart. Attach the pin through the slots.

Variation

Make the pin portion of your card out of fabric. Layer a piece of fleece or felt between two pieces of fabric cut in any shape you choose, and use a running stitch to sew around the edges.

p.s.

Each time you make a card you're especially fond of, run it through a copy machine before sending it. Stick the copy in your idea file, and it'll be there to remind you what you did and how you did it next time you want to try something similar.

Designer: Deborah Randolph Wildman

By blending efficiency and artistry, you can easily create large quantities of personalized card-and-envelope packets that make beautiful handmade gifts.

What You Need

8 pieces of card stock or handmade paper, each measuring 23 x 35 inches (59 x 90 cm)

11 pieces of text-weight paper, each measuring 23 x 35 inches (59 x 90 cm)

Thin piece of cardboard measuring 4³/₄ x 5¹/₄ inches (12 x 13.5 cm)

Strips of text-weight paper measuring 11¹/₂ x 6 inches (29 x 15 cm) (You'll need one strip per gift pack; we've provided a "recipe" for making up to 22.)

Raffia or ribbon

Ruler

Pencil

Bone folder

Glue

Clean rag

Tape with backing (available at craft stores and framing shops)

HAND-TORN NOTE CARDS
(makes 112 cards)

1

Stack the card stock neatly, and mark 5-inch (12.5 cm) intervals along both of the 35-inch (90 cm) edges of the stock.

2

Align the ruler along one set of marks, and use it as a guide to carefully tear one or two pieces of stock at a time along the ruler's edge (see figure 1). Move the ruler down to the next set of marks, and repeat the process until all of the paper is torn into 5 x 23-inch (12.5 x 59 cm) strips.

Figure 1

3

Divide the torn strips into several stacks, and mark two 9-inch (22.5 cm) intervals on each. (You'll have one 5-inch [12.5 cm] interval left over.)

4

Use the ruler as you did in step 2 to tear the stock at the 9-inch (22.5 cm) marks, creating stacks of 5- x 9-inch (12.5 x 22.5 cm) pieces. (See figure 2.) (You'll also end up with a stack of 5-inch [12.5 cm] squares. Set them aside for another project [see the P.S. on page 120].)

With the bone folder, fold the 5- x 9-inch (12.5 x 22.5 cm) pieces in half to create your note cards.

HAND-TORN ENVELOPES
(makes 110)

1

Stack the text-weight paper neatly, and mark 6¹/₄-inch (16 cm) intervals along both of the 35-inch (90 cm) edges of the paper.

2

Align the ruler along one set of marks, and use it as a guide to carefully tear one or two pieces of paper at a time along its edge (following the same procedure illustrated in step 2 above). Move the ruler down to the next set of marks, and repeat the process until all of the paper is torn into 6¹/₄- x 23-inch (16 x 59 cm) strips. (You'll have a 3³/₄- x 23-inch [9.5 x 59 cm] strip left over. Set it aside for another project.)

3

Mark the new strips at two 10¾-inch (27 cm) intervals.

4

Use the ruler to tear the paper into 6¼- x 10¾-inch (16 x 27 cm) pieces (see figure 2). (Again, you'll have a small strip of paper left over that you can set aside for another project.)

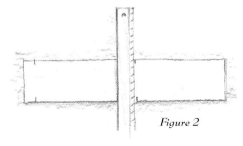

Figure 2

5

To fold the pieces into envelopes, lay the strips in a stack lengthwise. On the top strip, measure in 2 inches (5 cm)

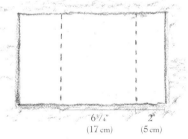

6¾" (17 cm) 2" (5 cm)

Figure 3

and 6¾ inches (17 cm) from the right-hand side, and lightly mark fold lines (see figure 3). Fold the top strip along the lines, and crease the folds with a bone folder. Use the first folded strip as a guide for folding the other strips (five to eight at a time).

6

Glue the envelopes together by unfolding the strips one at a time, lay-

ing them out lengthwise again, and running a thin bead of glue along the edges of the third panel (see figure 4). Fold the panel back up to form the envelope pocket, and use a clean rag to press the edges together and wipe off any stray glue that squishes out the sides. (Don't despair if the glue doesn't make the pocket stick together com-

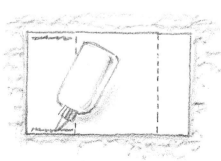

Figure 4

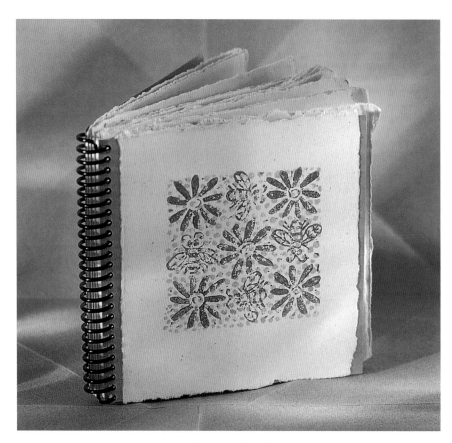

Mini-notebook made with leftover scraps

pletely at first. After you've made a stack of eight or so envelopes, use the rag to firmly squeeze all of the edges together at once, which should seal them up.)

7

Insert the thin piece of cardboard into each envelope before the glue is completely dry to make sure the pocket will seal in a way that accommodates your cards.

8

Apply a thin strip of tape with backing to the inside of each envelope's closure flap, leaving the backing on until you are ready to seal the envelopes.

Packaging the Packets

1

You can either use the plain note cards (which is fine, especially if the paper you created them from is distinctive) or embellish them in some way (stamping, stenciling, etc.) before putting them into packs.

2

Stack four note cards on top of five envelopes, and wrap the set in the strip of $11^1/_2$- x 6-inch (29 x 15 cm) paper.

3

Position the fifth note card on top of the pack, and tie the package up with raffia or ribbon.

p.s.

Here's a wonderful way to make use of the 5-inch (12.5 cm) squares left over from the card-making part of this project. Take them to a local copy shop and have them spiral bound into a mini-notebook or journal with a card-stock back and cover. Glue one square on the front, and cover it with decoration.

Designer: Susan L'Hommedieu

This is a card that sticks around (sorry, we couldn't resist). The design on the front is a custom-made magnet the recipient can pluck off and keep.

What You Need

Card stock folded into a card or a blank card

Image from a glossy, heavyweight magazine cover, or your own photograph

Scraps of card stock

Self-stick magnetic strip (available in rolls at craft stores)

Craft knife or scissors

Pencil

Glue

Rubber cement

1

Carefully cut around the edges of the image you want to showcase.

2

To reinforce the image, lay it on a scrap of card stock, trace around it, and cut out the traced image, cutting 1/8 inch (3 mm) inside the outline. Glue the reinforcing paper to the back of the image.

3

Using another small piece of card stock in a color that coordinates with the image, cut a square piece to frame the image (as the white card stock does in the project shown), and glue it to the card.

4

Cut an appropriate length of magnetic strip, peel off the backing, and attach the strip to the back of the image.

5

Use rubber cement on the other side of the strip to attach the magnet to the card. Since rubber cement is effective but not permanent, the recipient will have no trouble pulling the magnet off the card.

6

This technique creates a neat, raised-image look. The recipient may never guess that it doubles as a gift to be removed and used. Be sure to add a note inside about your creation's magnetic quality!

Designer: Kimiko Cards

What better way to relay a heartfelt "get well" than to send a steaming cup of tea on a card? You can adapt this clever concept to suit a variety of situations. A small packet of flower seeds poking out of a pot, for example, would be perfect for "happy spring" or "new beginnings."

What You Need

Card stock folded into a card or a blank card

Small piece of solid-color paper

Small piece of patterned, decorative paper

1 tea bag

Pencil

Ruler

Scissors or craft knife

Glue

1

Measure and cut a rectangle from your solid color piece of paper that is approximately $1/2$ to $1/4$ inch (1.3 cm to .6 cm) smaller than the front of your card. Glue the piece to the front of the card.

2

Using the template shown in figure 1 as a guide, cut a teacup out of the patterned paper.

3

Glue the teacup to the lower part of the colored paper, adhering all but the top edge of the cup.

4

Tuck the tea bag into the cup, and glue the label to the top right-hand corner of the colored paper.

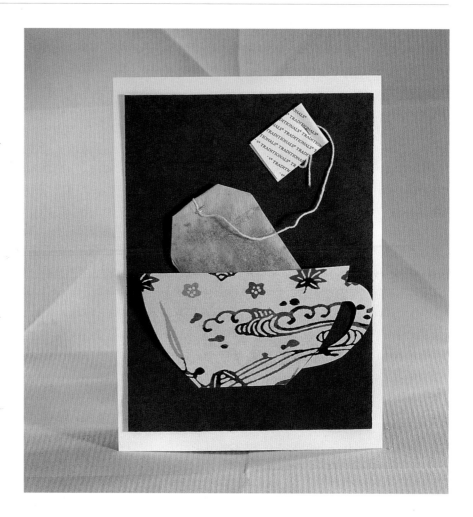

Variation

Replace the tea bag label with one of your own—a personalized tag that spells out your card's message.

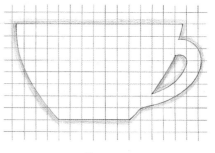

Figure 1

Sure, a handmade envelope is likely to catch its recipient's eye. But the United States Postal Service reports that those who really want to make an impression slap mailing labels and messages on everything from coconuts to kids. Here's a partial list of unlikely objects people have mailed as avant-garde "cards."

- Shoes
- Stuffed animals
- Driftwood
- Buckets
- Baby dolls
- Sacks of food
- T-shirts
- Fossils
- Brooms

And, as we said, coconuts and kids. Coconuts have long been popular among tropical vacationers as a mailable novelty. But kids?

Considered the most precious of cargo, small children have, on occasion, been shipped as parcel post between relatives. According to postal records, the children were personally cared for by mail carriers throughout their journeys.

☞ In 1914, a father had his young child mailed from Stillwell to South Bend, Indiana, after gaining custody from the mother. The mother placed the child in a container marked, "Live Baby," and paid 17¢ for postage.

☞ Four-year-old May Pierstroff was sent via parcel post in 1914 from her parents in Grangeville to her grandparents in Lewiston, Idaho. She was assessed by the chicken rate, for a total mailing cost of 53¢—much cheaper than train fare.

☞ Two children were mailed by their mothers to their fathers, who were tending machinery inside a plant during a factory strike in Tennessee in the 1930s.

The United States Postal Service now forbids the mailing of children.

THE BEACH

LARK BOOKS
50. COLLEGE ST.
ASHEVILLE, NC 28801

Contributing Designers

LINDA ANDERSON creates greeting cards, note cards, and more through her company, Wall/Flower Papers, 616-751-5666.

When not sending out greeting cards, BRIGID BURNS explores an ever-changing use of materials—primarily photography, collage, and mixed-media works on paper. Co-owner of Iris Photo/Graphics, addicted traveler, and an active, exhibiting artist, she has been a resident of Asheville, North Carolina, for the past 24 years. You can reach her at brigidburns@earthlink.net.

BARBARA BUSSOLARI is a retired Massachusetts high school teacher now living in the mountains of North Carolina. For the past 20 years, she has designed, made, and sold cards using handmade and hand-decorated papers and handwoven material. She is now exploring and expanding into paper jewelry.

PEI-LING BECKER is a paper collage and mixed-media artist who focuses on new applications for traditional Oriental art forms, colors, and symbols. Her work has received numerous awards and has been exhibited at galleries and centers throughout the United States, including the Kennedy Center and Lincoln Center.

ANNIE CICALE, former chemical engineer, became an artist when she decided to get serious about her career. She has a BFA in printmaking and an MFA in graphic design, and has taught art from the elementary school to the university level. She has been on the faculty of 17 international calligraphy conferences, and teaches workshops throughout North America.

MARGARET DESMOND DAHM lives in Asheville, North Carolina, where she runs a typesetting business with her husband and hand prints silk screen designs.

STEPHANIE ELLIS earned a BFA from the University of North Carolina at Charlotte, then relocated to Asheville, North Carolina, where she pursues her interests in painting and making handmade paper, journals, and cards. Recently, she has also begun to combine her work in painting and paper arts with the screen-printing process.

KATE HARPER is a self-made greeting card designer and publisher whose accounts have included Barnes and Noble, Borders Books, Tower Records, and Papyrus. In 1995, she was nominated for the greeting card industry's prestigious Louie Award. For the past decade, she has taught a class entitled "The Art and Business of Greeting Cards" to various groups, and her business has been featured in publications including *San Francisco Examiner* and *Nation's Business*.

KERRY HARVEY-PIPER is an English artist who has been designing and making cards for several years. She sells her work to shops and galleries in the United Kingdom and the United States. She has four children, a cat, a rabbit, a pet rat, three goldfish, and a very understanding husband.

DANA IRWIN is an artist who has custom designed and illustrated cards for many years. Her artwork has appeared in many nationally distributed books and magazines. She lives in Asheville, North Carolina, with her two dogs, two cats and her accordion in a very tolerant neighborhood.

KIMIKO CARDS is a small, handmade greeting card company in Berkeley, California, that ships its creations nationwide. Visit their website at www.kimikocards.com.

LYNN KRUCKE lives in Summerville, South Carolina, with her husband and daughter. She has long been fascinated with handcrafts of all types, and her favorite projects incorporate elements from more than one craft.

MARDI DOVER LETSON lives in Asheville, North Carolina, with her husband, Kellett, her son, Austin, and her dogs, Moses and Shelby. She operates a business creating handmade invitations, announcements, and greeting cards; call 828-253-4833.

SUSAN L'HOMMEDIEU, an avid gardener, enjoys sharing with others the knowledge and pleasure she has gained through gardening. She teaches a perennial flower garden course, is a free-lance garden writer and photographer, and gives workshops on card making with pressed plants. She has accumulated an admittedly totally excessive amount of paper, plant tidbits, and visually interesting items with the hope that she will eventually find time to make them all into cards.

CAROL PALLESEN works in her Reno, Nevada, studio, Silent Hand, as a calligrapher and book artist. She travels the United States teaching card, book, and calligraphy classes; it's her favorite thing to do. To reach Silent Hand, call or fax 775-329-6983.

HELEN ROBINSON is a designer and (occasional) artist who lives and works in Asheville, North Carolina.

LISA SANDERS has designed apparel for 14 years for major brand names. She has traveled all over the world and is currently a freelance designer working in apparel, home furnishings, and crafts in the New York City area. She enjoys exploring different techniques and translates her sense of design from one medium to another with ease.

ALLISON STILWELL is a Rhode Island designer who is constantly making things with stuff. She spends most of her time creating with fibers.

TRACY PAGE STILWELL creates dolls, quilts, painted furniture, and mixed-media projects. She is also known as a teacher, student, and curator, and can often be found in the garden.

TERRY TAYLOR is a multitalented artist whose work ranges from beading and lamp making to gilding and the pique-assiette mosaic technique. He allows bits and pieces of many art forms to influence his one-of-a-kind cards.

NICOLE TUGGLE combines bookbinding techniques with her passion for mail art to create unique letters and gift items. She uses her art as a means of communication, emotional release, and to celebrate the simple act of giving.

SANDY WEBSTER, an artist currently working in mixed media, received her BFA from Western Carolina University and is presently completing her MFA. Her works have appeared throughout the United States in publications and juried and invitational exhibitions. Sandy has taught, lectured, and juried fiber-related workshops and exhibits throughout the United States, Canada, and Australia.

DEBORAH RANDOLPH WILDMAN is an artist and organic gardener living on a farm in the Blue Ridge Mountains of Floyd, Virginia. She hopes to share with others the inspiration and nourishment she finds in the natural world through her work in art and gardening.

CALLIGRAPHERS who created the proposal postcards on page 50

W - Paul Maurer

I - Carl Rohrs

L - Denis Brown

L - Denys Knight

Y - Stan Knight

O - Ewan Clayton (and his class)

U - Mike Kecseg

M - Ward Dunham

A - Thomas Ingmire

R - Marsha Brady

R - Larry Brady

Y - Sheila Waters

M - Marcy Robinson

E - Annie Cicale

? - Peter Thornton

Index

Acknowledgments

I may get the handmade thank-you cards out yet, but for now, let me acknowledge those who helped this book along its way: Ruthanne Kah of M'Press Cards in Asheville, North Carolina, who put us in touch with many of the designers; Annie Cicale, for hours of helpful counsel, much inspiration, and many cardmaking connections; artist Karen Charatan, who shared lettering tidbits and ZIG marker samples; James H. Bruns, historian at the National Postal Museum and author of *Mail on the Move*, who helped with much of the sidebar trivia; Nicole Tuggle who, in addition to contributing card designs, lent her expert hands for the how-to photos; and my father, Don Gilchrist, a haunter of used bookstores who provided some timely research assistance!